You <u>Enter</u> the Kingdom of God based on the Nature of Your Spirit.
You <u>Inherit</u> the Kingdom of God based on the Character of Your Soul

UNDERSTANDING

The Difference Between
Your Spirit and Soul
Nature vs. Character

I0105898

Everest John Alexander

Unless Otherwise Stated All Scripture References
Are From the New King James Version of the Bible

Other References Are From:
New International Version (NIV)
New Living Translation (NLT)
English Standard Version (ESV)
Berean Study Bible (BSB)
New American Standard Bible (NASB)
Amplified Bible (AMP)
Christian Standard Bible (CSB)
Holman Christian Standard Bible (HCSB)
Contemporary English Version (CEV)
Good News Translation (GNT)
GOD'S WORD® Translation (GWT)
International Standard Version (ISV)
Weymouth New Testament (WNT)
Modern English Bible (MEB)

Paperback ISBN: 978-1-963922-02-8
Hardback ISBN: 978-1-963922-04-2
Ebook ISBN: 978-1-963922-03-5

Dedicated to the Chosen Few Among Whom Are...

Loraine Alexander
My Wife, My Hero

Ishmael Andrew Alexander
Elisha Jade Alexander
Our Children, My Inspiration

Sherry and Felicia
Family By Choice

Troy, Diane, Lori, Debbie
Who Led me to Christ

Apostle Rick Kendall
Pastor Paul Kendall
Bishop Winston Freckleton
Fathers of the Faith

Richard Seechan
Mentor & Friend

Pastor Lalloo Harricharan
Prophet of God

Dirk & Carol Richards
Faithful Ambassadors of God

Table of Contents

Introduction

This book is a **non-fiction** literary work explaining the design, function, and purpose of the Human Spirit and the Human Soul, including their similarities and differences.

The introduction directly below is an imaginative **work of fiction** which, hopefully illustrates the very real purpose of this book.

* * * * * * *

"Shut up! Shut up! Anna screamed, bolting down the stairs with her mom in hot pursuit.

Tears streamed down her face as she railed against her mother.

"How do you know that? Can you see the future now?!" Anna challenged her mom as she entered the living room.

Catching up to her daughter, Barbara pleaded, "Sweetheart, I'm your mother, I want the best for you! Trust me, this will not end well, it's my job to protect you, even from yourself."

"I don't need your protection, I'm a grown woman," Anna retorted, arms akimbo, head jutting forward as if to drive home her point.

"You're eighteen! You've barely begun to live!" Barbara countered.

"How could things have gone so wrong?" Barbara thought to herself. "We brought her up in church, knowing the ways of the Lord, now she's just going to…."

"You have no idea what's going on with my life and how I feel," Anna shouted, interrupting her mother's thoughts.

"Only *I* know the real me, and I need to be my authentic self right now." Anna's voice was firm but her gaze faltered just a little, betraying some inner doubt.

"Real me, authentic self… *who are you?*" "You sound like one of those idi…, misguided kids on social media." Barbara caught herself, her words stumbling out of her mouth as she moved closer to her daughter trying to re-establish some semblance of the intimacy they once shared.

"Now, that's just insulting," Anna snarled, pulling away from her mother. "You're saying I'm too **dumb** to know myself and *you* know me better! *Right!!?*"

Barbara made a deliberate effort to calm her voice as she responded, "Annie, sweetie, I may not have lived your life, but I've known you since before you were born, and more importantly, God knows you, and He said…"

"Oh, here we go again, ***Thus saith the lord!***" Anna interjected, rolling her eyes.

"You can mock all you want, but the truth will stand the test of time." Barbara offered… her arms outstretched, as though pleading for some re-connection with her daughter.

"Listen," Anna declared, stepping away, "you can preach all you want but it won't change what I feel in my **soul** and know in my **mind**."

I'm going to do this!" She grabbed the keys off the rack and angrily bolted out the door.

Barbara ran after her, shouting for her to come back and not radically alter her life.

Anna furiously backed the car out of the driveway and peeled down the asphalt, leaving her mother in tears of frustration on the sidewalk.

The vehicle disappeared into the night as Barbara thought to herself, "you feel in your *soul* and know in your *mind*… oh baby, you haven't got a clue."

"You don't even know the difference between your **spirit** and your **soul**. And now you're about to make the biggest mistake of your life."

"Oh God, I wish there was some way I could explain…"

1

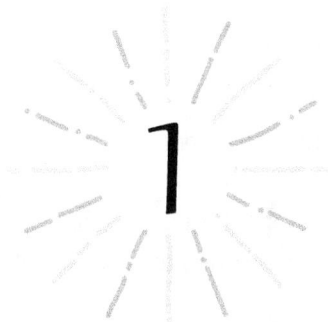

Man: A Limitless Revelation

To distinguish between your spirit and soul, we must first acknowledge that God designed human beings like Himself... A Trinity.

"God said, let us make humans in our image, in our likeness." Genesis 1:26 (GWT)

God made us like Himself, three in one, one in three.

God is:

The Father
The Word
The Holy Spirit

Humans are:

The Spirit
The Soul
The Body

As is the Creator, so is His Creation.

"For there are three that bear witness in heaven: the Father, the Word, and the Holy Spirit; and these three are one." 1st John 5:7

"I pray God your whole spirit and soul and body be preserved blameless unto the coming of our Lord Jesus Christ." 1st Thessalonians 5:23 (KJV)

The Bible confirms Human Beings are designed as a trinity, similar to our Creator.

Man is multi-faceted, he is spirit, he is soul, he is body.

Man is a spirit
Man is a soul
Man is a body

Anything less and he would not be a Human Being as created by God. He would be something else.

Let me explain:

For decades we have been taught that man *is* a spirit who *has* a soul and *lives* in a body.

This is a popular teaching in the Body of Christ but is only partially true.

With great respect to every Bible Teacher and Preacher who teaches this doctrine, it's really not 100% accurate according to Scripture.

After studying and teaching the word of God for over 35 years I've come to realize the significance of man being designed just like his Triune Creator.

We can say that God is the Father, who has the Son and operates through the Spirit… and that would be partially true but would it be 100% accurate? No, it wouldn't.

The full truth is:

God *is* The Father
God *is* The Son
God *is* The Holy Spirit

Anything less and He would not be God.

God is each One by Himself and all Three together.

Man is similar.

God created human beings as He is, three in one and one in three, each equal to the other.

Man is the Spirit
Man is the Soul
Man is the Body

Don't take my word for it, look at your Bible.

(And please forgive me, Sisters, I'm using the term 'Man' instead of Human Beings only because it's easier to write)

3 Levels of Identity

The Bible teaches, Man is a Spirit:

In Genesis 1:26 "God said, let us create man in our own image after our likeness." (KJV)

The word "likeness" in Hebrew is "d@muwth" (pronounced dem-ooth) and means "resemblance or similitude."

The **World Book Dictionary** defines resemblance and similitude as "to look like and to have the same essential qualities of."

To be created in the likeness of God means to be created to look like God and to have His essential qualities.

According to John 4:24, God is a Spirit, so to look like God and to have His essential qualities means to look like a spirit and have the essential qualities of a spirit.

What does that make Man? It makes Man a spirit.

So, the Bible confirms that Man is a spirit.

• • • • • • • •

The Bible teaches, Man is a Soul:

As we study the difference between the spirit and soul, it's important to understand that the soul and the mind are one and the same thing.

The mind is the soul. The soul is the mind.

In Genesis 2:7 "soul" is translated from the Hebrew word, "Nephesh" and among other things means, "mind, activity of mind."

This clearly suggests the connection of the soul and the mind.

Genesis 2:7 says, And the LORD God formed man *of* the dust of the ground, and breathed into his nostrils the breath of life; and man became a living soul.

So, man was created a physical creature (he was formed from the dust of the ground) also a spiritual creature (God breathe His breath of life into the physical man) then man took on a mental aspect (a soul).

He became a mental creature, self-aware and began operating on the mental level, together with the physical and spiritual.

He became complete and triune like his Creator.

The Biblical number 3 represents divine completion.

In the New Testament, the Greek word for 'soul' is 'psuche' from which we get our English words; psychic, psychology and psychiatry, all pertaining to the mind.

This further supports that the soul and the mind are one and the same thing.

The spirit is the inner-most part of a man, usually referred to as the heart, and the body is the outer-most part we see, sometimes called the flesh... so what is the soul?

The soul is the mind. The soul is the mental aspect of a human being.

The three aspects of a Human Being can be describes as:

Spirit = Heart
Soul = Mind
Body = Flesh

The Body belongs to the Physical/Natural Realm.

Both the Spirit and Soul belong to the Spiritual Realm.

The terms Soul and Mind are interchangeable because they are one and the same.

Most people, In their confusion, use the word "soul" when they really mean "spirit."

We hear people say all the time, "Body, Mind and Soul" but that terminology is not scriptural.

The Bible says, "I pray God your whole spirit and soul and body be preserved blameless." 1st Thessalonians 5:23 (KJV)

This scripture verse plainly shows that the soul is **not** the spirit and it is **not** the body… if it's not the spirit and not the body, what is the soul?

It is the mind.

Humans are made up of Body, Mind, and Spirit, so the soul must be the mind.

The Body is the outer man
The Soul is the inner man
The Spirit is the inner-most man

So, according to Scripture, the soul and the mind are one and the same.

Having established that, let us now see what the Bible says about man being a soul.

Genesis 2:7 says, "Man became a living soul," (KJV)

The bible did NOT say, he had a soul or he took possession of a soul. It clearly said he *became* a soul.

You can check the Hebrew meaning of the word "became" and it means just that, "became."

The word "soul" from the Hebrew "nephesh" also means "the person, the individual, the man himself."

Other Bible versions say, "…man became a living creature or a living being."

This leaves no doubt that the soul is the actual person and not just something he has or owns.

The French scientist and philosopher, René Descartes, wasn't incorrect when he asserted "I think, therefore I am"

He's stating that it's your mind, your ability to think, to be self-aware which makes you a person.

When Romans 13:1 says, "Let every soul be subject unto the higher powers," does it mean, only your *soul* must be subject to the higher powers, not your body or your spirit?
Of course not.

God is saying the **total you** must be subject because you and your soul are one and the same.

When He says "soul" He means *you, the entire person* because you *are* a soul.

So, the Bible confirms that Man is a Soul.

● ● ● ● ● ● ● ●

The Bible teaches, Man is a Body:

"And God formed man from the dust of the ground."
Genesis 2:7 (KJV)

Once again, the Bible did *not* say *"man's body"* was made from the dust of the ground, it said... *"Man"* was made from the dust of the ground.

I like the **Good News Translation**, which says, "Then the LORD God took some soil from the ground and formed a man out of it." Genesis 2:7

This leaves no room for misinterpretation, God formed a man from the soil, not his body... *A Man, a Human Being.*

The word "Man" in Hebrew is "Adam" (pronounced aw-dawm) and also means **"person."**

God made *"a person"* from the dust of the ground.

Not just his body... *Him.*

Your body is more than what you live in; it forms an integral part of who you are.

Your psychological state is significantly influenced by your physical condition.

When a woman's body goes through menopause, is it just her body, or does *she* go through menopause?

Have you ever been slapped in the face? Did you say, "oh that's alright, they didn't slap me, just my body?"

No, of course not, that person didn't just slap your body... they slapped *you!*

*They assaulted your **person**!*

If a boy is castrated, will he grow up to be the same man as if he was physically whole, or would he be a different person?

If you were born a different ethnicity, would your perspective on life be the same or would you be a different person?

Your physical body is a vital part of who you are.

If you're a black person reading this book right now, stop and consider: If you were born with white skin, blond hair, and blue eyes would you be the same person you are today?

No... of course, you wouldn't.

You wouldn't just be a person with white skin... You would be a **white person...** *and vice versa!*

The sum of all your experiences as a white person is what would make you into the person you are today.

Now, don't misunderstand me, as far as our basic humanity is concerned we are all the same.

God created one race on the earth - Human - and we are all brothers and sisters as far as creation is concerned.

The Bible literally says, "From one man he created all the nations throughout the whole earth" (Acts 17:26) that means there is no place for racism in the Kingdom of God... *at all!*

However, right now we're just discussing how our physical being impacts our identity.

As far as this is concerned, our physical make-up definitely influences our psychological identity.

In conversation, when referring to groups of people do we say, "people with white skin" and "people with black skin?"

No... we say "white people" and "black people" because we

instinctively know that our physical appearance informs who we are as people, as individuals, as human beings.

As a child, the color of your skin and all your other physical attributes contribute significantly to the person you grow up to become. Whether you are tall, short, fat, skinny, etc. all play a part in the development of your psyche.

A 7-foot-tall man would have a totally different outlook on life if instead, he was a little person 4 feet 5 inches tall.

He wouldn't be the same person!

I'm not saying he would be less in any way, I'm just saying he would be a different person.

Let me bring that comparison home to you.

If the ex-basketball player, Shaquille O'Neal was born in the body of actor Peter Dinklage and vice-versa, would they both be the same people we know today?

If Peter Dinklage was a 7-foot-tall black guy would he be the same Peter Dinklage we know today???

If Shaquille O'Neal was a 4' 5" tall white guy would he be the same person he is right now???

Would they both have the same personality?

Of course not!!!

What if you were born deaf or blind, would you be exactly the same person you are today? *No, you would not!*

Your experiences as a person who was deaf or blind would significantly contribute to the person you became.

So don't let anyone tell you that your body is just something you live in… *it's not!*

The condition of your physical self is a vital part of the corporate you.

Paul, the Apostle said, "We shall be changed. For this corruptible must put on incorruption." 1st Corinthians 15:52, 53 (KJV)

Read that again carefully, the Bible says, *"We shall be changed"* but it's referring to *our **bodies**.*

When the Bible says corruption must put on incorruption it's specifically referring to our physical bodies.

In the Rapture the only thing that changes is our bodies yet the Bible says *we* shall be changed.

Obviously, the Bible is saying a change in your body is a change in you as a person because you and your body are one.

The bible teaches that man is a physical being just as much as he is a spiritual and mental one.

'Man' was made from the dust of the ground, not just his body.

So, the Bible confirms that Man is a Body.

Church Tradition vs. Bible Doctrine

The design of Man is threefold.

He is a triune being like his Creator, three in one and one in three.

You are more than just a spiritual being, you are equally a mental being and equally a physical being.

God obviously considers our spirit, our soul, and our body to be of equal value and importance.

Why else would He inspire Paul to pray that our, whole spirit… *and* soul… *and* body be preserved blameless, without any distinction between the three? (1st Thessalonians 5:23)

I know I'm going against traditional church teaching here but my job is to teach the truth according to biblical doctrine not according to church tradition nor popular opinion.

The teaching that man is a spirit, who has a soul, and lives in a body began to be taught in order to highlight the importance of being led by our born-again spirit and not by our flesh.

This was necessary back then, but the problem is, we have gone so far east, we've ended up west.

In trying to teach something good we have inadvertently made a doctrinal error.

We indeed need to be led by our born-again spirit and not

---

by our flesh but what we ought not do is to minimize the importance, significance, and value of our body and soul in the process... which is exactly what we've done.

I've heard well-meaning Christians seriously say they don't need to read any other literature except the Bible... well that's just ignorance in full bloom, isn't it?

In much of the Body of Christ, there seems to be little regard for feeding the mind with good mental food, to cultivate a well-rounded intellect.

Paul, the Apostle said, "For in Him we live and move and have our being, as also some of your own poets have said, 'For we are also His offspring.'" Acts 17:28 (KJV)

In preaching the Gospel to the Greeks, Paul used his knowledge of Greek Poetry to establish a common bond so the Greeks would be more open to his Gospel message... *that's wisdom!*

As an effective Minister of God, Paul understood the importance of feeding his mind by reading and studying more than just the Holy Scriptures.

Let's illustrate this with an example:

It's so easy to quote scriptures that condemn homosexuality when we're speaking in generalities but how do you minister to someone struggling with homosexuality if that person is your friend or family member?

What if it's your own son or daughter, brother or sister, how do you deal with it?

The bible is clear that practicing homosexuality is wrong but when you care more about someone's well-being than just winning an argument, you need to do more than simply quote scriptures at them.

People need to know you understand and care about them as a person, so they can trust you and know you have their best interest at heart.

How can someone feel understood if you don't have a clue as to what they're going through?

Take the hypothetical situation of *'Claude'* who's been diagnosed with the medical condition known as AIS.

Androgen Insensitivity Syndrome (AIS), formerly known as, Testicular Feminization.

This is when a person who is genetically male is resistant to male hormones, resulting in having some of the physical traits of a woman, but the genetic makeup of a man.

In complete AIS, the penis and other male body parts fail to develop, which results in a boy physically appearing like a girl at birth.

Such individuals, like Claude, may grow up with serious sexual identity issues, compounded by society's warped attitude toward human sexuality and gender.

Claude may genuinely be searching for meaning to his life and in his quest for understanding, may have gravitated toward a homosexual philosophy and lifestyle.

Now up comes **Brother Christian** who has been taught that he is a spirit who simply has a soul and lives in a body, so he never paid much attention to educating himself intellectually and developing his mind outside of established church doctrine.

He has no clue that medical issues like AIS even exist and sees things strictly in black and white.

So, Brother Christian is thinking, "Claude is a homosexual and the Bible condemns homosexuality as SIN, therefore, Claude needs to REPENT or burn in hell!"

Well, it's true that Claude does need to repent... but repent of what, exactly?

Does Claude even understand what repentance is?

Has the Gospel of God's Grace ever been explained to Claude in a way he can understand?

Claude may never have had a real opportunity to repent because no Christian has ever understood his condition enough to show him any compassion.

Never having received compassion, Claude may never have felt the safety of trusting any Christian person enough to drop his guard, open up and receive the message of the Gospel of Jesus Christ.

Proverbs 11:30 says, "He who wins souls is wise."

It makes just as much sense to flip that around and say, "you have to be wise to win souls".

What's my point?

Developing your mind or soul is just as important as your spirit in obeying the great commission to evangelize the world for Jesus Christ.

If you don't have the correct understanding of your soul and don't place accurate value on your mental self, and you don't invest quality time developing yourself intellectually you may find yourself ill-equipped to obey Jesus' commands about winning souls for the Kingdom of God.

Peter was a simple fisherman who through the power of the Holy Spirit preached on the Day of Pentecost and won 3,000 souls to Christ, (Praise God) but when God wanted to communicate the power and truth of His Gospel to billions through all ages, it was the **educated and intelligent** Paul who He entrusted to write most of the New Testament... not Peter.

What about your body?

Would so many Christians be plagued by obesity, diabetes, heart disease and stroke if we understood the importance, significance, and intrinsic value of our physical selves?

Would so many Believers be involved in illicit sex if they understood their bodies were more than just something they lived in?

If they understood its intrinsic value of being a house for the Creator of the Universe to live in?

"Don't you know that your bodies are part of the body of Christ? Is it right for me to join part of the body of Christ to a prostitute? No, it isn't!"

"Don't you know that a man who does that becomes part of her body? The Scriptures say, "The two of them will be like *one person.*" 1st Corinthians 6:15-16 (CEV) **(Bold/Italics Mine)**

The Bible teaches that when you join *your body* to someone you become *one person.*

The Bible teaches that the body and the person are one and the same.

Just as it did in Genesis 2:7 when it said, God made a person from the dust of the ground.

I think the Bible is very clear on teaching that we are equally spirit, soul, and body and that each part is as important and valuable as the other two parts.

Man is a spirit
Man is a soul
Man is a body

He is each one and he is all three… just like his Creator.

The teaching that man is a spirit who has a soul and lives in a body is only *partial* revelation and not 100% accurate revelation.

I'm not saying that I've got the last or best revelation on this matter either.

No one has the full revelation on anything while we're still here on earth.

The only time we'll get the full revelation is after we get to Heaven.

While we're here, we know in part, we see in part, we understand in part, but then shall we know even as we are known. (1st Corinthians 13:12)

God is a limitless revelation and He made us just like Himself, in His image, in His likeness, so isn't it wisdom to acknowledge that Man also is a limitless revelation and all we know about ourselves is just a small degree of all there is to know?

There is so much to discover about ourselves, we're only just scratching the surface of the wealth of the knowledge of who we are, as regenerated Children of the Living God.

So, according to Genesis 2:7 man is made up of three components: the Dust of the Ground, the Breath of Life, the Living Soul.

1. **The Dust of the Ground** - Body - Flesh - Physical Man
2. **The Breath of Life** - Spirit - Heart - Spiritual Man
3. **The Living Soul** - Psyche - Mind - Mental Man

A perfect trinity just like his Creator who said, "Let us make man in **our image** and **our likeness.**"

Man is a limitless revelation.

2

Dividing Asunder

"For the word of God is living and active, sharper than any double-edged sword, piercing until it divides soul and spirit." Hebrews 4:12. (ISV)

In illustrating the power and precision of God's word, the writer says it divides soul from spirit, suggesting that the spirit and soul are very closely identified with each other.

Just how close are your spirit and soul?

In the verse above, the word "soul" is the Greek word "psuche" (pronounced psoo-khay) and means "breath".

The word "spirit" in Greek is "pneuma" (pronounced pnyoo-mah) and means "a current of air."

How's that for similarity? One is a breath and the other is a current of air.

At first glance, they seem to mean the very same thing and in a sense they do.

Is there any real difference between a breath and a current of air?

The World Book Dictionary says a breath is a vapor and a vapor is "something without substance."

So, the soul can be described as something without substance.

What can we learn from this statement?

The human soul is real, it has being but no physical properties or substance, which simply means that it's not tangible, it can't be experienced by the five senses, and in this regard, it's the same as the spirit... from a physical perspective they're both intangible.

The human spirit is called "a current of air."

What is a current of air?

Air (oxygen/nitrogen) is synonymous with life and a current is defined as a flow or stream.

So, in this context "a current of air" can be described as "a stream of life."

What is the human spirit? A flow or stream of life.

When someone is born again, the Holy Ghost recreates that person's spirit and reconnects that spirit to God, so the divine life of God can flow into and flow through that person.

God's divine life flows into and flows through a person's spirit.

That's how God designed Human Beings.

God designed the human spirit to be a conduit for Him to flow into and dwell, and flow through and bless.

That's why the human spirit can be described as a flow of life. It is a conduit for the Spirit and Life of God to flow into and flow through.

The human spirit is the interface that connects Man to God, allowing divine communication to take place.

Your spirit allows you to communicate with God.

It is the component God created from a portion of His own Spirit, which allows humans to relate to God.

The human spirit can feel what God feels, understand what God means and choose to act in agreement with God.

The human spirit is the seat of emotions, intellect, and will as they relate to God and the spirit realm.

The following scriptures support this:

The Bible says:

"My spirit hath rejoiced in God my Savior" Luke 1:47
"I am a woman of a sorrowful spirit." 1st Samuel 1:15

The human spirit is capable of feelings, therefore....

The spirit has emotions.

The Bible says:

"Nor can he know them, because they are spiritually discerned" 1st Corinthians 2:14
"But there is... a spirit [of intelligence] in man, And the breath of the Almighty gives them understanding." Job 32:8 (AMP)

These verses show that the spirit is intellectually capable, therefore....

The spirit has intelligence.

The Bible says:

"For God is my witness, whom I serve with my spirit." Romans 1:9
"With my spirit within me will I seek thee early." Isaiah 26:9

These verses show that within the human spirit there is volition, the capacity to choose, therefore....

The spirit has a will.

What about the soul?

We just saw that the human soul is intangible, made up of the same ethereal material that the spirit is made up of but how does it differ from the spirit?

The Bible says:

"My soul shall be joyful in the LORD." Psalms 35:9

"My soul is exceedingly sorrowful." Matthew 26:38

These verses show us that the soul can feel, therefore....

The soul has emotions.

The Bible says:

"Marvelous are Your works, And that my soul knows very well." Psalms 139:14
"That the soul be without knowledge, it is not good." Proverbs 19:2 (KJV)

This shows us that the soul is intellectually capable, therefore....

The soul has intelligence.

The Bible says:

"Truly my soul silently waits for God." Psalms 62:1
"Let every soul be subject to the governing authorities." Romans 13:1

To wait or be subject to, indicates the capacity to choose, which leads us to acknowledge that the soul is capable of volition, therefore....

The soul has a will.

What does this mean?

It means that the human soul is also the seat of emotions, intellect, and will, but primarily as they relate to other human beings and the natural realm.

In summary here's what we have:

Definition, Function, and Purpose of the Human Spirit:

The human spirit is the **God-conscious** mechanism in man.

It's the seat of emotions, intellect, and will primarily as they relate to God and the spirit realm.

The human spirit is synonymous with a person's inner-most nature.

The condition of a person's spirit is the condition of their nature and their nature determines their eternal destiny. *(Details in chapter 4)*

God designed the spirit to make humans conscious of God, to make us aware of the One who created us, and to provide a means of communication with Him.

The human spirit harmonizes with the spirit realm and receives and transmits impulses of a spiritual nature.

It allows man to talk to God and hear from God.

It is a stream of life, a conduit for God to flow into and through us.

This is the purpose of the human spirit... to be an interface between man and God, allowing God to indwell and empower us and to provide an efficient, accurate means of relating to and communicating with Him.

The Human Spirit corresponds to the Holy of Holies in the Jewish Tabernacle of the Old Testament.

The Bible describes we who are Born Again as the Temple of God.

"Do you not know that you are the temple of God and that the Spirit of God dwells in you?" 1st Corinthians 3:16

As God's temple, our spirit is the Most Holy Place where the presence of God abides.

As a born again Christian, the presence of God in the Person of the Holy Spirit takes up residence in your spirit, making it the Holy of Holies on Earth for God to inhabit.

Definition, Function, and Purpose of the Human Soul:

The soul is the **Self-conscious** mechanism in man.

The human soul or mind is synonymous with a person's character.

The condition of your soul or mind determines the quality of your character. *(Details in chapter 5)*

The soul provides the connection between the spirit and the body.

God designed the human soul to make man aware of his spiritual self on one end and his physical self on the other.

The soul is the perfect interface between the spiritual and the physical dimensions.

It communicates with the human spirit on one end and with the human body/brain on the other.

It harmonizes with the mental realm and receives and transmits impulses of a mental nature.

For instance, it allows human beings to communicate with each other by putting thoughts and emotions into words and sharing those words orally or orthographically.

This is one aspect of the soul's purpose... to allow effective communication between human beings but it goes further than this.

We'll explore this further in the next chapter.

3

The Perfect Interface

Not only does the Human Soul allow communication between human beings, but it also communicates with the Human Spirit.

This is the very reason the spirit and soul are so closely aligned. They are designed to perfectly interface with each other.

When God speaks to our spirit He doesn't speak Arabic, English, or Hmong; He speaks *the language of God (The original language He spoke to Adam and Eve in the Garden of Eden)*.

According to Genesis 11, earthly languages are a result of God's judgment on sinful men for rebellion at the Tower of Babel, so all human languages are born out of confusion as a judgment for rebellion.

When God came down in the cool of the day and spoke with Adam and Eve in the Garden, what language did He speak?

It wasn't any of the languages we speak today because none of them existed.

God spoke His original divine language to His first Children and I believe He uses the same language to speak to His Children today.

Your born again spirit understands the language of God perfectly so when God speaks to you, your spirit understands exactly what God said in His own divine language.

Your soul then interprets the information into your native tongue so it makes sense to you intellectually.

Through the interface of your soul, your brain becomes fruitful with the knowledge of your spirit.

So you proclaim, "God said such and such to me."

Not realizing that an extremely delicate and technical transfer of information from one dimension to another just occurred, all because of the function of your soul.

The purpose of the soul apart from human to human communication is to interface with the spirit, interpreting communications from God, and making intellectual sense, so we can take effective action.

God inhabits the spirit realm and we inhabit the natural realm, for communication originating in the spirit realm to be received and acted on in the natural realm, there must be some mechanism linking both realms and providing a conduit for such communications to travel through.

Such is the purpose of the human soul... to interface between the spiritual and the natural realms.

It links your spirit with your body... the spiritual dimension with the natural dimension.

On one end, your soul interfaces with your spirit and on the other, it interfaces with your brain.

The human brain is a remarkable device.

It's divided into 3 main parts or levels, the Cerebrum, the Cerebellum, and the Brainstem.

The Cerebrum is the largest and uppermost part, divided into left and right hemispheres which interpret hearing, vision, touch; and controls learning, emotion, etc.

The smaller Cerebellum lies under the Cerebrum and coordinates muscle movement, maintenance of balance, and posture, among other things.

The Brainstem is situated right at the very bottom and connects the Brain with the Spinal Cord.

It controls body temperature, heart rate, breathing, sleep cycles, digestion, etc.

(More on the brain in a subsequent book on the Physical Body)

Divine Communication

It's important to note that under normal circumstances when your spirit wants to communicate with God, communication is filtered through your soul.

Your soul interprets the communication from your spirit into your native language and the cerebrum of your brain initiates speech.

Of course, God being who He is, really listens to your spirit (your heart), so He knows exactly what you mean, regardless of the words you say.

This operation is suspended when you pray in tongues.

The manifestation of praying in tongues is simply your born-again spirit, speaking directly to God in His own divine language.

1st Corinthians 13:1 explains that there are languages of Men and languages of Angels… human languages and divine languages.

This explains why Christians may sound completely different from each other when praying in tongues, it's because even though we're all conversing with the same God, there are multiple dialects of heavenly languages available to speak.

1st Corinthians 13:1 refers to plural, "languages" of Angels, or what I describe as multiple dialects of divine language.

So, when a born-again Christian prays in tongues, it's simply our spirit communicating directly with God in a dialect of His own divine language.

That's why the bible says, "If I use an unknown language in my prayers, my spirit prays but my mind is useless."
1st Corinthians 14:14 (CEV)

When you pray in tongues, it's the operation of one intelligent spirit communicating directly with another intelligent Spirit, without the need for any mental understanding or translation... that's all.

You **speak** in tongues to men - You **pray** in tongues to God... one needs an interpretation, the other does not.

This biblical perspective should help clarify the issue of when interpretation of tongues is needed and when it's not.

At this point, let's reiterate the soul and the mind are one and the same.

The soul is the mind, the mind is the soul.

The mind consists of three components: Intellect, Emotions, Will.

The Intellect -   The ability to think
The Emotions - The ability to feel
The Will -   The ability to choose

These three aspects of your mind work together to facilitate your decisions, actions, and lifestyle.

3 Levels of Your Mind

There are three levels to the mind, the conscious, the subconscious, and the unconscious.

The word "sub" means "under" so the subconscious mind is what lies beneath, in other words, it forms the foundation for your conscious mind.

The unconscious lies even deeper and contains the hidden memories of childhood experiences, forming the beliefs, fears, and insecurities that influence our present behavior without us even realizing it.

The content of your subconscious and unconscious mind, which together I call the **non-conscious mind**, forms the root of your thoughts, emotions, and will.

The root of how you think, feel and choose.

Paul, the apostle said, "Be renewed in the spirit of your mind." Ephesians 4:23

In this verse, "mind" means thoughts, emotions, and will.

The English dictionary says the "spirit" of something is "the vital principle that gives it life."

So, "the spirit of your mind" can be considered "the vital principle that gives life to your thoughts, emotions, and will."

I believe what Paul describes as the spirit of your mind is really the content of your non-conscious mind.

This is what needs renewing, not just your conscious thoughts and emotions but also what gives life to them, what feeds them.

What feeds your conscious mind is the content of your non-conscious mind.

The non-conscious mind contains the vital principle upon which your conscious thoughts and emotions are based.

This vital principle significantly informs how and why we think and act the way we do, forming the basis for our Philosophy of Life.

Our Philosophy of Life is the sum of our conscious and non-conscious mind and consists of our Metaphysical and Ethical Paradigms.

Our Metaphysical Paradigm is our understanding of how the world is designed and operates.

Our Ethical Paradigm is our understanding of how we should think and behave in that world.

Summed up in one word, this is our... Worldview.

And this is what Paul is actually asking us to change...
Our Worldview.

"Do not be conformed to this world, but be transformed by the renewing of your mind." Romans 12:2

"Be renewed in the spirit of your mind." Ephesians 4:23

Change your worldview.

Change how you perceive and interact with the world around you.

It is the very reason why both Jesus and John came preaching to Israel saying, "Repent for the kingdom of God is at hand."

They were saying to Israel, change your worldview. Stop being slaves and prepare to become Kingdom rulers.

Exchange your worldly mentality for a kingdom mentality because another great Exodus is coming.

The difference is, this Exodus is spiritual, not natural.

When God used Moses to deliver Israel from Egypt, they instantly went from being slaves to being a free people in preparation to becoming Kings and Priests of God.

In the days of John the Baptist, when Jesus came, he began preparing Israel for another great Exodus… deliverance from Caesar's government to God's Government.

Deliverance from under the oppressive rule of the enemy to the liberty of submission to God's divine authority.

God is telling us Christians the same thing today, "Repent for the kingdom of God is here and it's already in you."

Change your paradigm and start thinking like Kingdom Rulers, not as slaves to sin, not as citizens of the world but as citizens of God's Kingdom.

Put on the mind of Christ.
You are more than conquerors.
You are overcomers through the blood of the Lamb and the word of your testimony.

He's telling us to adopt a new Philosophy of Life, a new Worldview by renewing our minds, both the conscious and the non-conscious mind.

This focus on the non-conscious mind is not strange when we consider that the word "mind" in certain passages of scripture is translated as "heart."

For instance, "Out of the abundance of the heart, the mouth speaks." Matthew 12:34

In this passage, the word "heart" doesn't refer to the spirit as it usually does but to the non-conscious mind, showing again how intimately close the spirit and soul are.

We become renewed in the spirit of our minds or renew our non-conscious mind by employing what I call, the 7 Biblical approaches to the word of God.

They are:

1. Read the word
2. Study the Word
3. Memorize the Word
4. Discuss the Word
5. Meditate the Word
6. Confess the Word
7. Practice the Word

The Bible says, "Faith comes by hearing, and hearing by the word of God." Romans 10:17

It's not just a one-time action but must be habitual to derive the full benefit from it.

Each of these 7 habits forms an integral part of renewing your mind.

1. Reading the word gives you information, which increases knowledge

2. Studying the word gives you explanation, which increases understanding

3. Memorizing the word gives you ammunition, which increases your protection

4. Discussing the word gives you new perspectives, which increases your perception

5. Meditating on the word gives you revelation, which increases wisdom

6. Confessing the word gives you manifestation, which increases your conviction

7. Practicing the word brings perfection, which facilitates dominion. (Perfection means Spiritual Maturity)

Practicing these 7 habits renews your mind, both the conscious and the non-conscious.

It is your renewed mind which allows you to effectively

demonstrate dominion.

Dominion is the authority and ability to rule God's creation, beginning with your own life.

Dominion is our ultimate purpose. As it was in the beginning so shall it be in the end.

In Genesis, God's primary command to the Human Race was… Have Dominion!

The more we renew our mind, the easier it is to hear the voice of our reborn spirit, which always agrees with God and wants us to walk in holiness and demonstrate dominion.

To complete the process from right thinking to right living we must understand that our body, our soul, and our spirit each has a will of it's own and a voice to express that will.

3 Levels of Your Will

Your spirit, your soul, and your body each has a will of its own and a voice to express that will.

A. The Voice of your spirit is your Conscience… Your Conscience tells you what is right and what is not.

B. The Voice of your soul is your Reason… Your Reason tells you what is intelligent and what is not.

C. The Voice of your body is your Appetite… Your Appetite tells you what is pleasurable and what is not.

A. Conscience distinguishes right from wrong.

B. Reason distinguishes sense from nonsense.

C. Appetite distinguishes pleasure from pain.

Illustration: Monday morning when your conscience - the voice of your spirit - tells you to get out of your warm, cozy bed, go shower, get dressed, and go to work or school, what does your body say?

Your body says I'm staying right here and continuing to sleep in this warm, comfortable bed for the next couple hours.

Your spirit and your body begin to oppose each other and conflict ensues with an eventual winner.

Let's break that down…

When your conscience says, "get up and go to work" it's stating what is *right.*

This is a workday and we are expected to be on the job or at school, we have a moral responsibility to be present at our place of work or institute of education, this is the **right** thing to do.

Your reason, which is the voice of your soul usually agrees with your spirit, saying, (in the case of work) we should get up and go to work because we have bills to pay and we need that salary at the end of the month.

This makes sense, it's the *intelligent* thing to do.

Your appetite, which craves comfort and pleasure, usually disagrees with your conscience and your reason and declares: I'm staying in bed and sleeping until I'm satisfied because it's the *pleasurable* thing to do.

Therefore, your spirit and soul have to gang up on your body and force you out of bed.

In any given situation, your spirit, your soul, and your body, will have something to say, and it is not uncommon to find them alternately opposing and agreeing with each other depending on the situation.

Which Voice Are You Listening To?

The will of your born-again spirit is always aligned with the will of God, so, the voice of your spirit - your conscience - will always guide you right.

The will of your body and mind... not so much.

That's why the Bible says, you need to renew your mind and kill the tendencies of your flesh.

The voice of your mind - your reason - will not always guide you into God's will because making sense is not the same thing as being right.

Intelligence does not equate righteousness or wisdom.

There are many educated intellects who either despise God or say He doesn't exist... God calls them both fools.

As an example, it made absolutely no sense for Moses to lead

Israel to the Red Sea with the entire Egyptian army behind them in hot pursuit... this was a trap of his own making.

However, it was the right thing to do because it's exactly where God wanted them, so He could display His mighty power in delivering them and eliminating Pharaoh's army once and for all.

It's always better to be right than smart.

The voice of your body - your appetite - will not always lead you into God's will either.

Make no mistake, your appetite is indeed necessary, otherwise, you would never feel hungry and eventually starve to death or you would never feel sexual attraction toward your spouse and without reproduction, the human race would become extinct.

So, your appetite is both necessary and good, the problem occurs when it is left unchecked and runs into excess or used in perverted ways for ungodly gratification.

It makes sense then, that we practice being led by our conscience - the voice of our reborn spirit - so that we consistently walk in God's divine will and continually demonstrate dominion.

This is how we experience the full manifestation of the abundant life Jesus came to give us.

"I came that they may have life, and have it in abundance [to the full, till it overflows]." John 10:10 (AMP)

Listening to, and obeying the voice of your reborn spirit - your conscience - is how you consistently walk in victory and success.

It's very important to note that this is true only for the Born

Again Believer.

A person who has *not* had their spirit regenerated by God and not had their nature divinely transformed, cannot depend on their conscience to always lead them right.

This is the very reason Jesus said you *must* be born again. (John 3:7)

It's only a renewed spirit and a transformed nature that will guarantee that you are led into the divine will of God.

The conscience of an unsaved person cannot be trusted, it will lead them right today and wrong tomorrow, in the will of God today and completely out of His will tomorrow.

This is so crucial that even when the conscience of a Born Again Christian leads them into the right ways of God it's still the voice of their soul - their reason - that has the last say on what they actually choose to do... this is called exercising "free will."

Our soul is the deciding factor - we must still use reason to choose to obey the will of our spirit in order to experience success and victory in life.

This struggle of our 3 wills, is a direct result of our progenitors eating from the Tree of the Knowledge of Good and Evil.

'Good and Evil' is not the same as Right and Wrong (Righteousness and Unrighteousness).

What is good may not always be right.

The natural condition of every unsaved person is to operate by the human standard of good and evil and not by God's standard of right and wrong.

A pure and profound sense of Right and Wrong is what eating from the Tree of Life would have given Adam and Eve.

They, however, ate from the Tree of the Knowledge of Good and Evil, and here we are today, the human race is still struggling as we attempt to live by our own human standards of good and evil, instead of God's standards of Righteousness and Unrighteousness.

The fact remains, that each part of you:

Your Spirit
Your Soul
Your Body

Each has a will and a voice to express that will:

Your Conscience
Your Reason
Your Appetite

The more we consistently listen to and are led by our born-again conscience the more we experience victory and success in this life and the better prepared we are to reign and rule with Jesus Christ when He returns.

In the following chapters, we will discuss how the condition of your spirit and soul affect your nature and character and how your nature and character determine *if* and *how* you enter heaven.

4

The Nature of Your Spirit

Your nature is determined by the condition of your spirit.

Your character is determined by the condition of your soul.

Your nature determines *if* you enter heaven.

Your character determines *how* you enter heaven.

If more Christians understood this simple difference, it would eliminate much confusion and division in the Body of Christ.

2nd Peter 1:4 says, "He has granted us His precious and wondrous promises, in order that through them you may, one and all, become sharers in the very nature of God." (WNT)

It is only through His promises that we share God's divine nature, therefore, people not covered by His promises do not share His nature.

People outside the Promise or Covenant of God do not share in God's divine nature but have mere human nature.

Since Adam was the first Human, we can refer to Human Nature as Adamic Nature and since human Sin began with Adam, we may refer to Adamic Nature as the Sin Nature.

So, going forward, we may refer to either the Sin Nature, Human Nature, or Adamic Nature… they're all the same.

Death is a separation.

If you separate a person's spirit and soul from their body, the body dies.

If you separate a person's spirit from God, their spirit dies.

It is the connection with God that allows His life to flow into a person.

No connection with God means no spiritual life, resulting in spiritual death.

This is exactly what Adam and Eve experienced the moment they ate the fruit of the Knowledge of Good and Evil.

God told Adam, the day they ate from that tree they would surely die… and they did.

They immediately died spiritually. Their spirits became

separated from God, so He could not flow into, nor live inside them.

They experienced spiritual death instantly and also began to experience physical death, which was fulfilled years later.

It's the same with Adam's descendants today, we're all born spiritually dead, separated from God and we begin to physically die the moment we're born.

We will eventually experience physical death because we are born spiritually dead.

We're born with our spirit separated from God, so His life cannot flow into us, this leaves us with just the Human or Sin Nature.

The condition of our spirit determines the condition of our nature.

A dead spirit (separated from God) results in a Sin Nature

A New Spirit - A New Nature

God created Adam perfect, pure and innocent, without the knowledge of Sin.

Adam was, however, given the choice to obey or disobey God and he chose to disobey God.

Man was created with his spirit like a blank slate, waiting to be imprinted on.

His choice to obey or disobey God would determine the imprint upon his spirit, whether righteous or unrighteous and sadly, he chose wrong.

When he chose to rebel against God's authority, his spirit was imprinted with the nature of rebellion and disobedience, the nature of Sin and Unrighteousness.

Since then, every descendant of Adam is born with that same Sin Nature of Unrighteousness with the natural result of rebellion and disobedience.

Who teaches a child to lie? No one, it's inherent in human nature.

It's very informative, the way God describes humans who are not yet born again.

He doesn't describe them in ambiguous terms, He's very clear.

He says..."At that time you were apart from Christ. You were foreigners and did not belong to God's chosen people. You had no part in the covenants, which were based on God's promises to his people, and you lived in this world without hope and without God." Ephesians 2:12 (GNT)

Before becoming Born Again human beings are...

1. Without Christ
2. Not among God's Chosen People
3. Have no part in God's Covenant Promises
4. Living in this world without Hope
5. Living in this world without God.

I can't tell you how many times I've asked some Christian person about the spiritual condition of a friend or family member and their answer is totally contrary.

It usually goes like this:

ME: "Is so and so saved?"

CHRISTIAN PERSON: "Well, they have a heart for God and attend church, so I don't know, maybe..."

Listen, reader, when it comes to Salvation there are no shades of grey, there is no ambiguity whatsoever.

A person is either Born Again or not, saved or lost, spiritually alive or dead, going to heaven or hell.

That friend or family member who is the sweetest, kindest, most generous soul you know, who wouldn't harm a fly... if they are **not** Born Again according to the Bible, they're presently on their way to Hell.

If they have not repented and believed the Gospel of Jesus Christ and confessed Christ as their Savior and Lord, then they are **NOT** Born Again and consequently under the wrath of God and will be sentenced to Eternity in the Lake of Fire.

Christian... this is not the time to be confused about this.

If you love that person you will do everything in your power to get them Right with God... NOW!

I don't mean beating them over the head with scriptures or dragging them to church with you.

I mean being a true friend to them, cultivating a real relationship, and interceding for them, asking God for the opportunity to share the Gospel with them, with the love and power of the Holy Spirit.

When God gives you that opportunity, you seize it with zeal and allow the Holy Spirit to work through you, bringing your friend or family member into the Kingdom of God with you.

That... is what real love looks like.

You, being tolerant of their sinful lifestyle and encouraging them to be rebellious against God with their worldly philosophies and contrary doctrines...*that is not love!*

The Bible really does encourage us to "love the sinner and hate the sin."

Jude 1:23 says, "Rescue others by snatching them from the flames of judgment (that's loving the sinner)... hating the sins that contaminate their lives (that's hating the sin)." (NLT)

To be effective in winning souls for Christ we must be clear on the actual condition of those we love, who are not yet born again.

The Bible says, "You used to be far from God. Your thoughts made you his enemies, and you did evil things." Colossians 1:21 (CEV)

Did you get that?

We were **enemies** of God before we were born again...
all of us.

The Amplified Bible spells it out when it details our condition before we were born again, it says, among these unbelievers we all once lived in the passions of our flesh, our behavior governed by the sinful self, indulging the desires of human nature without the Holy Spirit and the impulses of the sinful mind. We were, by nature, children under the sentence of God's wrath, just like the rest of mankind. (Ephesians 2:3)

Thank God however, the scriptures did not stop there, it went on to say, but God, being so very rich in mercy, because of His great and wonderful love with which He loved us, even when we were spiritually dead and separated from Him because of our sins, He made us spiritually alive together with Christ for by His grace — His undeserved favor and mercy — you have been saved from God's judgment. (Ephesians 2:4-5)

The Bible says, before we were saved we were spiritually dead.

Some of you reading this right now believe your unsaved loved one is "almost" a Christian... I'm here to tell you, *there is no such creature!*

No such human being exists.

There is a clear line between the living and the dead... you are either one or the other.

Listen to what I'm about to tell you very carefully… there is only one Hell, not two or three.

Everyone who is not saved is going to spend eternity in Hell, whether they were a mass murderer, serial killer, child molester, or whether they were a church-goer, coached the soccer team, volunteered at the Boys and Girls Club, or preached in the pulpit for 50 years.

If you listen to Jesus discuss wolves in sheep's clothing then you know there are people who have preached for decades who are not saved at all and going to hell.

You must be Born Again!

That's why King David cried out to God, "Create in me a clean heart, O God; and renew a right spirit within me. " Psalm 51:10

That's why God promised through the prophet Ezekiel, "A new heart also will I give you, and a new spirit will I put within you." Ezekiel 36:26

It's why Jesus explained to Nicodemus, "you must be born again." (John 3:7)

To be born again is to be given a new spirit or heart and a new nature.

It's this new spirit and new nature which guarantees you entrance into heaven.

That's why the Bible confirms, "He saved us... by the cleansing of the new birth (spiritual transformation, regeneration) and renewing by the Holy Spirit." Titus 3:5 (AMP)

What Does 'Born Again' Mean?

First, let me tell you what it is not.

Becoming born again is <u>not</u>...

- Getting Water Baptized (Infant or Adult)
- Any Roman Catholic Sacraments
- Joining a Church
- Converting to the 'christian religion'
- Changing your ways
- Stop sinning
- Having a supernatural or religious experience
- Getting miraculously healed or delivered
- Anything that involves your own human efforts

Becoming Born Again is a miracle which God performs on the inside of you, all by Himself, without your help.

You simply trust Him to do it by surrendering your will to Him... that's it.

To clear up any misunderstanding of what becoming Born Again is, I've attempted a detailed explanation of the exact process below.

Bearing in mind this is my clumsy human attempt to explain the most beautifully sublime, powerfully miraculous work of God in a human being.

The process of becoming Born Again goes like this...

First, you hear the Gospel of Jesus Christ.

What is the Gospel?

It is the good news that even though you were born spiritually dead, separated from God and on your way to Hell, Jesus Christ took the judgment for all your sins upon Himself and died in your place on the cross at Calvary.

He was buried and rose from the dead in victory three days later so you could receive His righteousness in place of your guilt and be reconnected to God and receive God's divine nature so you can live with Him forever in Paradise.

To receive this miracle all you need do is believe it is true and repent.

That's the Gospel in a nutshell.

You hear it and when you do, God gives you the grace to receive it.

Receiving it, means you accept it as being true.

As you accept the message, it becomes a Seed planted in your spirit.

That Seed is the Word you heard.

This Word-Seed contains the Nature of God because God and His Word are one; they cannot be separated. The bible says, "...The word was God." (John 1:1)

Omnipotence is part of the Nature of God, therefore, His Word has the power to create anything.

The Genesis Chapter One creation account confirms this when it explains that both the Father and the Holy Spirit were present, but nothing happened until God spoke.

Only when His Word was released did creation begin.

It is the divine power in God's Word which created the universe.

It is this same divine power in God's Word which re-creates your spirit.

Let's continue illustrating the born again process.

The creative power of God in the form of His Word is planted in your spirit as a Seed.

God then gives you the faith to act upon that Word-Seed.

You act in faith by believing and trusting the Gospel message and confessing Jesus Christ as your Savior and Lord.

While you're declaring what you believe to God, you're surrendering your will to Him, trusting Him to perform His miracle inside you.

That's how you apply your faith in this situation.

The words you actually say is called the "Prayer of Salvation" and might go something like this:

Prayer of Salvation

Lord Jesus, you said in Revelation 3:20 that you're standing outside the door of my heart, my life, and knocking for me to let you in.

I now make the decision to open the door of my heart, my life, and let to you in.

I believe you are the Son of God, you died, you were buried, and on the third day, you rose from the dead in victory and glory.

Come in to my life Lord Jesus and make your home in my heart, forgive me and cleanse me from all my sins and make me a child of God.

Lord Jesus, I accept you alone as my Savior and my Lord. Thank you. Amen.

● ● ● ● ● ● ● ●

When you pray these words from your heart, it acts as a catalyst germinating the Word-Seed, releasing the life of God within you.

This process is such that the faith you apply acts on the God-Seed cracking it open, allowing the life of God to flow out into your spirit.

If you plant a natural seed in the soil a similar thing happens.

When you plant a corn seed into the ground, the heat and moisture of the earth causes the seed to swell and burst open, releasing the life of the corn within.

As new life springs out, a brand new plant is created from that seed in the soil.

The Bible says God's people are, "Trees of righteousness, The planting of the LORD." Isaiah 61:3

In the born again process, your spirit is like the earth, your faith and words are like the heat and moisture, which cause the Word-Seed to burst open releasing God's divine life within you.

As this new life flows out of the Word-Seed, it completely engulfs your formally dead spirit transforming it.

Where there was death there is now life. Where there was old, there is now new.

"When this has taken place, then that which was said in the Writings will come true, Death is overcome by life," 1st Corinthians 15:54. (BBE)

Your old spirit ceases to exist and a brand new spirit is recreated in its place. You have become a new creation in Christ.

"Therefore, if anyone is in Christ, he is a new creation; old things have passed away; behold, all things have become new." 2nd Corinthians 5:17

The life of God is synonymous with the nature of God, so as

His life flows into you, His Nature is released.

Receiving the life of God, therefore, is the same as receiving the Nature of God.

You now have a new, divine nature.

"He has given to us the greatest and precious promises, that through these ye may become partakers of [the] divine nature," 2nd Peter 1:4 (DT)

God is Holy, which means, to be unique, other than everything else, sanctified, consecrated, and set apart as extremely special.

This is what God is and this is what you have become when you share His nature…you are Holy.

You have become a different type of human being, one of God's New Creations.

You are unique, different, changed from natural to spiritual, from death to life…

You are Born Again!

In the Born Again Process, the Holy Spirit recreates a brand new spirit within you, reconnecting you to God, so the life of God can flow into you, imparting His divine nature.

2nd Peter 1:4 says, "These are the promises that enable you to share his divine nature." (NLT)

The promises referred to here, are outlined in the New

Covenant, which you enter when you repent and believe the Gospel of Jesus Christ.

The New Covenant is the 6th of 7 Major Biblical Covenants discussed in the Bible.

It's a divinely orchestrated, legally binding contract between God and the Human Race mediated by His Son, Jesus Christ.

When someone receives Jesus as their Savior, they enter into God's New Covenant and become an heir to the promises of God which He made to Abraham.

The Bible says, "Christ paid the price so that the blessing promised to Abraham would come to all the people of the world through Jesus Christ and we would receive the promised Spirit through faith." Galatians 3:14

The Bible says, "The promises were spoken to Abraham and to his descendant... referring to one. That descendant is Christ. You are all God's children by believing in Christ Jesus. If you belong to Christ, then you are Abraham's descendants and heirs, as God promised." Galatians 3:16, 26, 29 (GWT)

God promised eternal salvation and earthly blessings to Abraham because Abraham trusted and believed in God.

God's promise to Abraham was re-established through Abraham's Heir, Jesus Christ, and consequently to everyone who believes in Jesus Christ today.

To "believe" in Jesus Christ does **not** mean to mentally acknowledge that He lived, preached and did miracles.

When the Bible says "Believe in Jesus Christ" it means to have a deep conviction in your heart that His Gospel is true and to respond to that Gospel (Good News) in faith.

The Gospel (Good News) is that even though your sinful nature and your sins have sentenced you to eternity in Hell, Jesus Christ has already been judged and died in your place and paid for all your sins with His own Life.

He was buried and three days later rose from the dead in glory and victory, then He ascended into heaven to be your Intercessor, praying to God for you day and night.

In doing this, He gave you the gift of salvation which is Eternal Life with God.

To receive this gift you simply believe the good news and repent.

Repenting is how you trust God to create the miracle of the New Birth within you.

The entire process of becoming Born Again, which we just explained must be precipitated by repentance.

What is Repentance?

Repenting is what you do *internally* before the Prayer of Salvation.

It's what's going on in your mind as you are confessing those words out of your mouth.

To repent means to change your perception of reality and see the truth as it actually is, then act accordingly.

The truth is, God loves you and wants the best for you and if you continue to live life on your own terms, based on your own understanding and abilities, you cannot achieve eternal success.

You must give up control of your life to God and submit your will to His greater will... *this is repentance.*

Whatever you're trusting in and relying on for eternal security, you have to give that thing up and embrace Jesus Christ alone as your Savior.

Receiving salvation is free, you don't have to work for it, nor can you earn it in any way, but *there is an exchange involved.*

Imagine you're holding a huge box with both hands and this box is filled with shiny stones that look great but have no real value.

Then someone comes along and offers you a beautiful Treasure Chest filled with genuine diamonds, rubies, gold and silver.

To receive this new Treasure Chest, you have to do two things:

1. You must first put down the useless box of stones already in your hands.

2. You must stretch out your empty hands and take hold of the Treasure Chest being offered to you.

This is what repentance is like... *it's an exchange.*

Before receiving Jesus as your Savior, your mind is already filled with some idea that gives you a sense of spiritual security.

That idea might be, "devotion to my religion will save me," or "if my good works outweigh my bad works, that will save me," or "God doesn't exist so there's no judgment, therefore, I don't need to be saved."

It doesn't matter what that idea is, it's exactly like that box of shiny stones, it appears to be valuable or valid but it's not, it seems like an intelligent argument but it's based on a lie... it's just a useless weight you're carrying around.

Now, here comes Jesus Christ offering you true salvation, represented by that Treasure Chest filled with real precious gems.

You must first put down the useless box of pretty stones in your hands, then stretch out your empty hands and take hold of the Treasure Chest being offered to you and possess it.

That's how you repent!

I knew a man over 30 years ago who firmly believed in reincarnation when the gospel was presented to him.

He believed that if he died he'd simply return to earth in a new body, but as the gospel was being shared, one scripture verse kept going through his mind, "It is appointed unto men, once to die but after this, the judgment." (Hebrews 9:27)

No matter how he tried, that scripture verse would not leave him alone.

Everything else explained to him that day made perfect sense, so finally, he gave up and submitted his will to God and confessed Jesus Christ as his Savior and Lord.

The key is... he had to completely give up the false belief that reincarnation could keep him safe from God's eternal judgment and he had to trust the finished work of Jesus Christ alone for salvation.

The moment that man did that, in the middle of his salvation prayer he felt a divine peace fill him, flowing from the top of his head down through his body, filling him with a sense of safety, peace and righteousness he'd never known before in his entire life, in that moment, he knew beyond any shadow of a doubt... he was saved.

He knew it!

It's been 35 years as of the writing of this book and he's still serving the Lord with passion and conviction.

It will be the same with anyone who truly repents and trusts Jesus Christ as their Savior.

Whether it's religion, good works, or whether someone is an Atheist who believes there is no God... for every human being, the beginning of repentance is to see the truth as it is, not as they wish it to be.

When someone makes the decision to repent, they must simply confess that decision to God (that's the Prayer of

Salvation) and God will take it from there.

Whether they repeat after someone or say their own prayer, it doesn't matter.

When they confess the truth that Jesus Christ has paid for their sins and they receive His free gift of salvation, the Holy Spirit will re-create their spirit and release the divine life and nature of God within them, transforming them from the inside out.

The Holy Spirit will begin to live inside them, continually imparting divine life into their spirit.

This is what becoming born again means and this is the direct result of repentance.

When someone repents and becomes Born Again the new spirit and new nature they receive, guarantees them entrance into heaven and eternity with Christ.

The Bible says, "For by one offering He (Jesus) hath perfected forever them that are sanctified." Hebrews 10:14 (KJV)

Did you get that? He perfected them… *forever!*

There is no re-doing Salvation, once you receive it… it's done.

Salvation is permanent and cannot be reversed, that's why God calls it Eternal Salvation.

"He became to all who obey Him the source and giver of eternal salvation." Hebrews 5:9 (WNT)

Furthermore, Jesus said, "My sheep hear My voice, and I know them, and they follow Me. I give them eternal life. **They shall never perish**, nor shall anyone snatch them from My hand. My Father, who has given them to Me, is greater than all. No one is able to snatch them from My Father's hand. John 10:27-29 **(Bold Type Mine)**

Jesus said, He gives His sheep eternal life and *they shall never perish."*

This tells me, either salvation is permanent or Jesus is a liar... I know which one I believe.

One of the reasons some Christians believe they can lose or give up their salvation is because they don't understand the difference between their spirit and their soul and consequently they don't understand the difference between their nature and their character.

In the following chapter, we will begin exploring the significance of building Christian character and how it affects our entrance into heaven.

5

The Character of Your Soul

In the previous chapter, we gave a detailed explanation of how our nature is determined by the condition of our spirit.

A regenerated, born again spirit gives us a new divine nature.

We showed that our new divine nature guarantees us entrance into heaven and eternity in the presence of God.

In this chapter, we'll give the same attention to the soul.

We'll explain how our character is determined by the condition of our soul and how the quality of our character determines, not *if* but *how* we enter heaven.

As your nature is synonymous with your spirit, so your character is synonymous with your soul.

The condition of your soul/mind determines the quality of your character.

We saw earlier that your mind or soul is composed of your intellect, emotions, and will.

Now, we'll take a look at what constitutes your character.

The word "Character" from the ancient Greek "Kharakter" means, "symbol or imprint on the soul."

Just as your nature is imprinted on your spirit, so, your character is imprinted on your soul.

The condition of your mind or soul determines the quality of your character.

Three Levels of Intimacy

There are 3 levels of intimacy in knowing someone.

1. Their Reputation
2. Their Personality
3. Their Character

You can know someone's reputation before ever meeting them, never having seen or heard them, you can still know a lot about them.

They could live on the other side of the planet and you can still know all about their exploits and accomplishments, their reputation having preceded them.

Knowing someone's personality takes a little more intimacy, it will become apparent as you spend time with them, getting to know them personally.

And the more time you spend with that person, the more you can see beneath the surface of their personality and discover their true character.

Reputation vs. Character

Your Reputation is people's opinion of you - Your Character is God's knowledge of you.

Reputation is external - Character is internal.

Reputation is built on perception - Character is built on authenticity.

Reputation is based on perceived facts - Character is based on actual truths.

Personality vs. Character

Your character and your personality are not the same but as your spirit and soul are intertwined, so are your character and personality.

This means they share some areas of similarity, so sometimes what is said of your character can also be true of your personality.

For instance, "Graciousness" is the quality of being benevolent, courteous, and kind, and it can equally describe your personality or your character.

Below are some differences:

Your personality consists of inherent traits and tendencies predominantly assigned from birth.

Your character consists of a set of attitudes, values, and characteristics acquired through experience.

Personality results from inborn predisposition - Character derives from learned behavior.

Personality is more or less permanent - Character can be changed.

Both personality and character may vary with different situations or circumstances.

As Christians, we are expected to live in such a way that our reputation, personality, and character all consistently align with the image of Christ, which is godliness and holiness.

In the early years of King Solomon, he was a perfect example of this type of integrity.

"When the queen of Sheba heard about Solomon's reputation with the LORD, she came to test him with difficult questions." 1st Kings 10:1 (ISV)

The Queen of Sheba knew of King Solomon's reputation even though she lived thousands of miles away and never met him.

After traveling to Jerusalem, meeting and spending time with him, the queen began to get familiar with his personality and verified what she heard about his reputation was true.

"She said to King Solomon, "What I heard in my own country about you and your wisdom is true!" 1st Kings 10:6 (GNT)

After investing more time with the King she finally declared, "May the LORD your God be praised because he favored you by placing you on the throne of Israel! Because of the LORD's eternal love for Israel, he made you king so you could make just and right decisions."1st Kings 10:9 (NET)

Her confidence in Solomon to make just and right decisions was born from knowledge of his character, not just his reputation or personality.

Solomon's reputation, personality, and character were all consistent with a godly man who accurately represented God.

The Queen of Sheba confirmed this by spending time with him verifying that his reputation and personality matched with his character and they all glorified God.

What is Character?

Character is the sum total of the learned qualities and characteristics that distinguish and define an individual.

The holiness of your character determines the godliness of your conduct.

Your character is the content of your moral self and is comprised of 7 major attributes.

Your character consists of your habitual:

1. Thoughts
2. Emotions
3. Motives
4. Intentions
5. Memories
6. Imagination
7. Judgments

How these components relate to ethics, defines the essence of your character, and their balance and relation with each other makes your character unique.

Let's look at each of them in more detail.

Thoughts and Emotions:

The great reformist, Martin Luther said, "You cannot keep birds from flying over your head but you can keep them from building a nest in your hair."

Such is your thought and emotional life.

You cannot keep random thoughts from passing through your mind but you can keep sinful or negative thoughts from making their home there.

Every word or deed begins with a thought and as such, we will be judged by Jesus Christ for every thought we choose to entertain.

It's why He admonishes us in His word, "Don't become like the people of this world. Instead, change the way you think. Then you will always be able to determine what God really wants-what is good, pleasing, and perfect." Romans 12:2 (GWT)

Just like our thoughts, random emotions continually pass through our souls, influencing how we perceive reality.

Our responsibility is to take control of our emotions and have them work for us and not against us.

The Bible reminds us "we live by faith and not by sight." 2nd Corinthians 5:7

It's a reminder that we are in control of our thought and emotional life and are not victims of them.

Thought and emotional manipulation is one of the chief weapons the enemy uses against us.

Demonic spirits can manipulate and deceive humans by implanting wrong thoughts and emotions in their minds.

These thoughts usually begin with the words "I", I'm or I'll and if you're not wary, you will accept the thought and make it yours.

You may think, "I'm such a failure, what's the point of trying, I'll just disappoint everyone again" and with this thought come feelings of unworthiness and self-pity.

You may accept these thoughts and emotions as your own and proceed to act on them, making them a self-fulfilling prophecy.

But remember, the original thoughts and emotions were not yours to begin with.

They were implanted by the enemy and because those two thoughts started with the words **"I'm"** and **"I'll"** you believed they were yours and acted accordingly, but only the action was yours, the original thoughts and emotions were not.

Paul, the Apostle, told Timothy to be gentle when correcting others, "That they may come to their senses and escape the snare of the devil, having been taken captive by him to do his will." 2nd Timothy 2:26

The Bible says people are taken captive by the devil to do his will.

How does he do that? How does the devil take someone captive to do his will?

He manipulates their thoughts and emotions, deceiving them into disobeying God and acting how he wants them to act.

It's our responsibility to discern the difference between our own thoughts and those implanted by the enemy and to act accordingly.

There's an incident between Jesus and Peter that clearly illustrates this.

The Bible recounts, "From that time Jesus began to show to His disciples that He must go to Jerusalem, and suffer many things from the elders and chief priests and scribes, and be killed, and be raised the third day."

"Then Peter took Him aside and began to rebuke Him, saying, "Far be it from You, Lord; this shall not happen to You!"

"But He (Jesus) turned and said to Peter, "Get behind Me, Satan! You are an offense to Me, for you are not mindful of the things of God, but the things of men." Matthew 16:21-23

Satan obviously planted thoughts in Peter's mind and Peter believed the thoughts were his own so he acted on them and began rebuking Jesus.

Jesus knew Peter's thoughts were **not** his own, not originating in Peter's mind, so He rebuked the source of the thoughts and not the vessel they came through.

He looked at Peter but said, "Get behind me **Satan**."

This was not an insult to Peter, it was a teaching moment where Jesus was demonstrating spiritual warfare to His disciples.

There are times you need to correct people's ignorance or bad attitude but there are times you need to address and rebuke Satan or demons directly.

Peter spoke contrary words to Jesus but Jesus knew the source of those words were thoughts that originated with the devil so Jesus directly rebuked the source of those contrary words... Satan himself.

The Bible says, "We are destroying arguments and all arrogance raised against the knowledge of God, and we are taking every thought captive to the obedience of Christ." 2nd Corinthians 10:5 (NASB)

We must habitually analyze our thoughts and emotions and not accept the enemy's counterfeits but take every thought captive to obey Christ.

We take every thought captive by; reading, studying, memorizing, meditating, discussing, confessing, and practicing the word of God until it becomes an indelible part of who we are.

We also need to fellowship with the Holy Spirit until we become intimately familiar with His voice, so when He speaks we can easily recognize and obey Him.

Disciplining our thought and emotional life is key to cultivating Christlike character.

Cultivating Christlike character pays huge dividends at the Judgment Seat of Christ.

Motivation and Intention:

Motivation and Intention are similar but not the same.

Motivation is what inspires or compels us to action.

Intention is what we plan to achieve from our action.

Motive is the reason for doing something - Intention is the result we desire from doing it.

When we stand before Jesus, we'll be judged not only by our thoughts, words, and deeds but by our motives and intentions as well.

Honorable motives inspire us to glorify God; dishonorable motives compel us to glorify ourselves.

One can do the right thing but for the wrong reason, negating any real spiritual benefit.

Jesus said, "So when you give to the poor, don't announce it with trumpet fanfare. This is what hypocrites do in the synagogues and on the streets in order to be praised by people. I can guarantee this truth: That will be their only reward." Matthew 6:2 (GWT)

Giving to be noticed by others has self-glorification as its motivation and self-promotion as its intention.

The Bible says, "God's word is living and active. It is sharper than any two-edged sword and cuts as deep as the place where soul and spirit meet, the place where joints and marrow meet. God's word judges a person's thoughts and intentions." Hebrews 4:12 (GWT)

Job's experience is an interesting example of motive and intention.

Job's intention was honorable but his motive was flawed.

Job was motivated by fear. This is indisputable because he plainly said so.

"The thing I greatly feared has come upon me, And what I

dreaded has happened to me. I am not at ease, nor am I quiet; I have no rest..." Job 3:25-26

Job was driven by a carnal fear of God's judgment falling upon him and his children.

The Bible says, "When they finished having their feasts, Job would send for them in order to cleanse them from sin. He would get up early in the morning and sacrifice burnt offerings for each of them. Job thought, "My children may have sinned and cursed God in their hearts." Job offered sacrifices for them all the time." Job 1:5

It's important to note, the Bible never said his children sinned during their feasts... he just assumed they might have and proceeded with his religious ceremony and sacrifices.

His motive - the reason for his religious zeal was a legalistic fear of God's judgment.

His intention, however, was pure. Job wanted to make sure he and his family were right with God and accepted by God

Job knew about God but he did not have an intimate relationship with Him, so as most people do, he assumed the worst about God and acted on this faulty knowledge.

Job knew about God by reputation but was not as familiar with His character.

At the end of the Book of Job after God finally revealed Himself to Job, he told God, "You asked, 'Who is this that questions my wisdom with such ignorance?' It is I—and I was talking about things I knew nothing about." Job 42:3 (NLT)

Job further said, "I had heard of You [only] by the hearing of the ear, But now my [spiritual] eye sees You." Job 42:5 (AMP)

These are Job's own words.

At the end of the book when God appeared and started rebuking everyone, Job finally confessed he was ignorant of God's character and was talking about things he didn't fully understand.

It's only after God revealed Himself to Job that he began having a personal relationship with Him based on accurate knowledge and understanding of who God really was.

God's revelation of Himself led Job to repentance, and this repentance purified his motives.

With his motivation purified and aligned with his intention Job now found himself in place to receive a double portion of God's blessing.

Here are some practical ways to help purify your own motives and intentions:

1. Saturate your mind with God's word
2. Cultivate a lifestyle of praise and worship
3. Place a priority on the truth, loving it above all else
4. Receive correction with humility
5. Treat the Holy Spirit as a real Person and make Him a vital part of your every day life
6. Know that the Holy Spirit is Almighty God, living inside you, conforming you to the image of Christ daily
7. Acknowledge the Holy Spirit in all you do and trust Him to help you renew your mind

Memory and Imagination:

Memory is the mental faculty of retaining and recalling past experience. However, your memory doesn't operate like a recording machine.

Memories are not step-by-step recordings of past events as most people assume.

They're constructed piece by piece when they're first retained and reconstructed every time they're recalled at a later date.

The molecular mechanisms involved in creating and maintaining memories incorporate simulating and imagining future experiences as part of their creation process.

That means your imagination actually plays a part in forming your memories... isn't it just like an Eternal God to design us in such a way that we use our future to help record our past.

The conclusion is that remembering is a reconstructive rather than a reproductive process.

Each time you remember an experience, that memory is a new construction of events and not a copy of the past.

How does this information help you live a godly life?

Let's press on and find out.

The Misinformation Effect

There's a famous study by psychologists, **Dr. Elizabeth Loftus** and **Dr. John Palmer** where participants viewed a video of a traffic accident and then questioned about it.

Participants were divided into two groups and asked a question:

Group A. "How fast were the cars going when they smashed into each other?"

Group B. "How fast were the cars going when they hit each other?"

Group 'A' gave higher estimates than Group 'B'

Furthermore, when asked sometime later if the video of the accident had broken glass in it, Group 'A' reported, yes, there was broken glass in the video, and Group "B" said no, there was none.

There was actually no broken glass in the video, showing that the wording of the questions distorted the viewers' memories of the event.

The wording of the questions led people to construct different memories of the same event.

Group 'A' who were asked the question with the word 'smashed' remembered a more serious accident than they had really witnessed.

The findings of the experiment were replicated worldwide,

and researchers consistently demonstrated that when people were provided with misleading information they tended to misremember... A phenomenon known as **"The Misinformation Effect."**

Satan has mastered the misinformation effect in order to manipulate people's memories to achieve his goals.

God the Father, told Jesus, you are My beloved Son in whom I am well pleased. (Mark 1:11)

Satan came after, tempting Jesus saying, if you are the Son of God make these stones bread. (Luke 4:3)

He left out the word, "beloved" because there was no way he was going to remind Jesus of what God said to Him.

The word "beloved" magnifies the love of the Father for His Son and God's grace toward His Children.

Satan did not want Jesus focusing on this, but of course, Jesus didn't fall for it and resisted Satan's temptation.

In the garden of Eden, God said to Adam and Eve, of all the trees in the garden you may freely eat.

When Eve recounted the matter to Satan who was working through the Serpent, she said, "of all the trees we may eat."

She forgot the most important word... freely.

That word typified the largesse of God toward His Children.

Through manipulation, Satan deceived Eve into forgetting the goodness of God in freely giving them everything and caused her to focus on the one thing He denied them.

Isn't that just like us today?

Forgetting everything God has graciously given us and focusing only on what we don't have.

This is the misinformation effect expertly articulated by Satan.

Fact vs. Truth

Even when we accurately remember negative experiences from our past, we still don't have to walk in defeat because of them.

You never have to accept defeat from the enemy because... **facts are temporary but truth is eternal.**

The devil may use something horrible from your past to try to intimidate and defeat you.

Pay him no mind, the severity of your sin is irrelevant, as a Born Again Child of God you are forgiven, sanctified, accepted and loved by God unconditionally.

Through the Apostle John, God says, "I am writing to you, little children, because your sins have been forgiven you for His name's sake." 1st John 2:12

You are forgiven.

The Bible says, "And such were some of you. But you were

washed, but you were sanctified, but you were justified in the name of the Lord Jesus and by the Spirit of our God." 1st Corinthians 6:11

You are sanctified (made holy).

"To the praise of the glory of His grace, by which He made us accepted in the Beloved." Ephesians 1:6

You are accepted.

"But God demonstrates his own love for us in this: While we were still sinners, Christ died for us." Romans 5:8

If Christ died for you while you were still a sinner, this means His love is unconditional.

You are unconditionally loved.

Facts may say you're a fornicator or adulterer.
Truth says you are holy, you are the temple of God.
(1st Corinthians 3:16)

Facts may say you're weak and give in to temptation easily.
Truth says you are an overcomer through the blood of the Lamb and the word of your testimony. (Revelation 12:11)

Facts may say you're afraid to go to sleep at night because of demonic oppression.
Truth says, you are more than a conqueror through Christ Jesus and you have been given power over all the power of the enemy and nothing shall by any means hurt you.
(Romans 8:37; Luke 10:19)

Facts may say you are sick and facing certain death.
Truth says you are healed and walking in divine health.
Truth says you will live and declare the works of God.
(1ˢᵗ Peter 2:24) (3ʳᵈ John 1:2) (Psalm 118:17)

Facts are temporary, they change all the time
Truth is Eternal… It Can Never Change!

No matter what the facts of your past or present are, let each
memory and every thought be filtered through the lens of Truth.

The Truth is… Whatever God's Word says about you!

The Power of Imagination

Imagination brings the future into the present and helps to
manifests the invisible.

Imagination is a powerful ability that's criminally underrated
and terribly misused.

The correct use of imagination is one of the most powerful
forces in the universe.

The power of imagination can impact the world and often does.

"I have a dream, that one day…" this statement sees the
invisible and brings the future into the present.

Someone built a global empire on the belief that…
"Dreams really do come true."

One does not, however, have to be a Dr. King, a Walt Disney, or a Mother Teresa to wield the immense power of imagination.

Simply imagine yourself in someone's shoes **before** you judge them… that's the correct use and power of your imagination.

"If you judge people, you have no time to love them" ~ Mother Teresa.

Selfishness is fueled by a lack of imagination.

If you cannot imagine walking in someone else shoes, your understanding of, and empathy for them will be limited by your lack of imagination.

A lack of imagination is one of the severest handicaps in all of human experience.

Imagination is something children have naturally mastered, so Jesus says to us, "I'm telling you, once and for all, that unless you return to square one and start over like children, you're not even going to get a look at the kingdom, let alone get in. Whoever becomes simple and elemental again, like this child, will rank high in God's kingdom." Matthew 18:3-4 (MSG)

Simple, elemental, full of wonder, and boundless in imagination… we must not only receive the Kingdom of God like a child but oftentimes we need to operate in the kingdom like children to be most effective.

The more powerful your imagination, the easier it is to see yourself in someone else's situation, experience their reality and act with empathy toward them.

The truth is, we'll all be judged by how we use our imagination.

"The LORD... saw that everything they thought **or imagined** was consistently and totally evil. And... said, 'I will wipe this human race I have created from the face of the earth." Genesis 6:5, 7 **(Bold Type Mine)**

God killed everybody on the planet because people were imagining evil too much ... *that's how important your imagination is.*

Even after the flood, as soon as men began to multiply on earth again, God found Himself in a similar situation.

"And the LORD said, "Behold, they are one [unified] people, and they all have the same language. This is only the beginning of what they will do [in rebellion against Me], and now no evil thing they imagine they can do will be impossible for them." Genesis 11:6 (AMP)

Nothing they <u>imagine</u> will be impossible for them to do... *God said that!*

Think about that for a minute.

God is saying about us human beings, if we can imagine it, we can do it!

This is not some light, pithy, dime-a-dozen motivational quote.

It's a cosmic truth out of the mouth of your Creator about you.

Your imagination is one of the most powerful forces at your command.

Jesus used His imagination to glorify God by maintaining a clear vision of His purpose and destiny.

The power of His imagination and conviction gave Him the courage and strength to literally go through Hell and emerge victorious on the other side.

The Bible says, "We must focus on Jesus... He saw the joy ahead of him, so he endured death on the cross and ignored the disgrace it brought him. Then he received the highest position in heaven, the one next to the throne of God." Hebrews 12:2 (GWT)

To 'see the joy ahead of him' Jesus had to use His imagination.

To a very large extent, it is the correct or incorrect use of your imagination that will determine the degree of your success or failure in life.

Faith is the substance of things hoped for, the evidence of things not seen. Hebrews 11:1

If it's not seen then you have to imagine it!

Faith is the power of your imagination founded and grounded on the Word of God.

Judgment:

The dictionary defines Judgment as, "the ability to make considered decisions or come to sensible conclusions."

God considers using sound judgment so important He devoted an entire Book of the Bible to it.

The Book of Proverbs opens with...

The proverbs of Solomon, the son of David, king of Israel:
To know wisdom and instruction, to perceive the words
of understanding, to receive the instruction of wisdom,
justice, **judgment**, and equity. Proverbs 1:1-3

The Bible says, "All Israel... feared the king, for they saw that
the wisdom of God was in him, to execute sound judgment."
1st Kings 3:28

Paul, the Apostle said, "For I say... to everyone among you,
not to think of himself more highly than he ought to think,
but to think with sound judgment." Romans 12:3

The message of the Book of Proverbs is simple... stop making
foolish decisions and start using sound judgment.

All other aspects of character culminate in this one thing...
using sound judgment.

The correct use of your thoughts, emotions, motives,
intentions, memory, and imagination all conclude with you
making sound judgments, resulting in godly conduct...
which is the purpose of cultivating holy character.

The next chapter explores the difference between the two great
end-time judgments, based on our Nature and Character.

6

Two End-time Judgments

There are two major End-time Judgments that individuals will experience.

There's a third judgment of Nations but in this book we'll only focus on the two end-time events for individuals.

They are:

1. **The Great White Throne Judgment**
2. **The Judgment Seat of Christ**

Both judgments take into account our Nature and Character but the first judgment deals primarily with Nature and the second judgment deals primarily with Character.

The Great White Throne Judgment

The Great White Throne Judgment is for the Unrighteous, for Sinners, Unbelievers, Non-Christians, anyone who has not had a faith-filled response to the revelation of God the Father through Jesus Christ or through Creation.

Everyone who is not saved, who has not been declared righteous by the Lord will be judged for their Human/Adamic/Sin Nature and their sinful choices, at the great white throne judgment.

Both their Nature and Character will be called into question.

Here's something that most people don't realize...

There are two levels of JUDGMENT and two levels of PUNISHMENT dispensed to a condemned sinner.

It's similar to the natural process of Law where a guilty criminal is arrested, jailed, and awaits trial, then after he's tried and found guilty, he's sentenced to a prison term.

In the Case of a Natural Criminal:

1. Preliminary Judgment is **Jail**
2. Final Judgment is **Prison**

In the Case of a Sinner (Spiritual Criminal):

1. Preliminary Judgment is **Hades (Hell)**
2. Final Judgment is **The Lake of Fire**

When a Sinner dies they go to Hades and await the Great White Throne Judgment. On Judgment Day they'll be officially tried and sentenced to spend Eternity in the Lake of Fire.

These Are the Two Levels of Judgment:

1. **Hades**
2. **The Lake of Fire**

These are two different areas of the Underworld.

Now, let's look at the two levels of Punishment for the Sinner.

The Bible says, "Then I saw a great white throne…. And I saw the dead, small and great, standing before God, and books were opened."

"And another book was opened, which is the Book of Life. And the dead were judged according to their works, by the things which were written in the books." Revelation: 20:11-12

The reason two sets of Books were opened, is to facilitate the two levels of punishment.

The Book of Life judges a person's Nature… it shows whether he's righteous or unrighteous, whether he's sentenced to Heaven or Hell.

The Books of Works (other books) are for judging a person's Character… they show his level of unholiness, which determines the severity of his punishment.

The Book of Life determines *where* someone spends eternity.

"Anyone not found written in the Book of Life was cast into the lake of fire." Revelation 20:15

The Books of Works determine the quality of punishment a condemned sinner receives.

"The dead were judged according to their works, by the things which were written in the books." Revelation: 20:12

Condemned sinners will experience different degrees of punishment for their evil works, which is based on the unholiness of their character.

An unrepentant child rapist, for instance, will not receive the same level of punishment as say the average 17-year-old who died without Christ.

Someone who devoted their whole life to doing good works but never accepted Jesus as their Savior will, unfortunately, go to hell but will not receive the same level of punishment as, for instance, an Adolf Hitler or a King Leopold II of Belgium, who reportedly was responsible for mass murders, rapes, and other genocidal atrocities, perpetrated on over 10 million African men, women, and children.

The concept of varying degrees of punishment for sinners may sound strange but is quite scriptural.

Jesus said, the scribes and Pharisees were hypocrites "who devour widows' houses, and for a pretense make long prayers. These will receive greater condemnation." Mark 12:40

Greater condemnation suggests a different degree of punishment.

Let's confirm this by looking at the actual Greek meanings of these words.

Greater - perissoteron - more abundantly, far more.

Condemnation - krima - the sentence of a judge, the punishment with which one is sentenced, damnation.

Jesus seemed to confirm this when He said, "People of Capernaum, do you think you will be honored in heaven? You will go down to hell! On the day of judgment the people of Sodom will get off easier than you." Matthew 11:23-24 (CEV)

Jesus here indicates that the people of both cities will go to hell but they will experience different degrees of punishment there.

This is because of another principle Jesus explained in scripture, He told Pontius Pilate, "The one who handed me over to you is guilty of a greater sin." John 19:11 (NIV)

According to Jesus, there are different degrees of sin, some are greater than others, this supports the concept of different degrees of punishment.

What these different degrees of punishment are, the Bible does not say but that they do exist is clear.

So, there are two levels of judgment for the unrighteous dead:

1. **Hades** - Where sinners are incarcerated until their Trial on Judgment Day

2. **The Lake of Fire** - Where sinners spend eternity after being sentenced

There are also two levels of Punishment for the unrighteous dead:

1. **Eternity Separated from the Benevolent Person, Presence, and Power of Almighty God**
2. **Varying Degrees of Punishment in the Underworld**

At the Great White Throne Judgment only condemned sinners are judged.

Varying degrees of punishment notwithstanding, every condemned sinner will spend eternity separated from God, burning in a lake of fire, being eaten by worms.

When describing Hell, Jesus said, "There 'the worms that eat them never die, and the fire that burns them is never put out.' Mark 9:48

Whether these "worms" are literal or symbolic, it is certain this experience will be quite horrendous.

So, even though there are differing degrees of punishment, please do not assume for one moment that any punishment in hell is tolerable... *it is not!*

The worst of society who have not repented will experience a greater degree of punishment but make no mistake, everyone in hell will burn for all eternity.

The Judgment Seat of Christ

Born Again Christians **will not** and **cannot** be judged at the Great White Throne Judgment because Jesus specifically said, "He who hears My word and believes in Him who sent Me has everlasting life, and **shall not come into judgment**, but has passed from death into life. John 5:24 **(Bold Type Mine)**

He then confirmed this when He said... **His sheep shall never perish.** (John 10:28)

There is, however, a separate judgment for Christians, which is really an evaluation of our service to God.

It's called the **Judgment Seat of Christ...** also referred to as, **The Bema.**

The noun "Judgment" and the verb "To judge" can be somewhat ambiguous.

For instance, there's a different implication between the two following statements:

1. You have been judged guilty of treason and sentenced to death.

2. We judge you to be a person of sound moral character and trust you completely.

The first judgment leads to condemnation because of guilt.

The second judgment is an evaluation of good character.

One leads to condemnation, the other to validation.

Simply using the word "Judgment" does not automatically lead to a negative experience.

Jesus said, "Judge not, that you be not judged." Matthew 7:1

This same Jesus said, "Judge with righteous judgment." John 7:24

Two different commands from Jesus, which on the surface seem to contradict each other, but which do not because God's Word never contradicts itself.

Jesus' first statement warns us not to condemn others, because we open ourselves to the same condemnation.

Jesus' second statement admonishes us to evaluate people and situations based on God's standard of righteousness, not our own.

However, in both statements, the same English word "Judge" is used.

Similarly, the word "Judgment" is also used in the two end-time events.

The **Great White Throne Judgment** is where and when sinners will face their final condemnation to the Lake of Fire.

The **Judgment Seat of Christ** is where and when Believers will be evaluated for their life's work in service to God.

"For we [believers will be called to account and] must all

appear before the judgment seat of Christ, so that each one may be repaid for what has been done in the body, whether good or bad [that is, each will be held responsible for his actions, purposes, goals, motives—the use or misuse of his time, opportunities and abilities]." 2nd Corinthians 5:10 (AMP)

The Judgment Seat of Christ is **not** a condemnation for having a sinful nature, nor for any sins committed.

It's an evaluation of how you performed as a Servant of Christ while employed by Him on Earth.

When you signed up to become a Christian you stepped into several different offices.

You became a Citizen of the Kingdom of God and along with Kingdom Citizenship you became:

1. A Son of God
2. A Servant of God
3. A Soldier of God

As a son, you have all the rights, privileges, responsibilities, and benefits of a child of the King of the Universe... *this is unimaginably glorious!*

The Bible says, "Since we are his children, we are his heirs. In fact, together with Christ we are heirs of God's glory. Romans 8:17

(If you're female, don't be put off by being called a son, because all Christians are also the Bride of Christ and Jesus is our Husband, even if we're male)

Plus, the Bible actually says, "In Christ there is neither male nor female for we are all one." Galatians 3:28

As a soldier, you became enlisted in the army of God and are expected to:

1. Be strong in the Lord and in the power of His might. (Ephesians 6:10)
2. Put on the whole armor of God (Ephesians 6:11)
3. Master your weapons of warfare (2nd Corinthians 10:4)
4. Fight the good fight of faith (1st Timothy 6:12)
5. Bear one another's burdens, and so fulfill the law of Christ. Galatians 6:2
6. Endure hardness as a good soldier of Christ (2nd Timothy 2:3)
7. Wrestle **not** against flesh and blood, **but** against principalities and powers, against the rulers of darkness and wicked spirits in heavenly places. (Ephesians 6:12)
8. And having done all… Stand! (Ephesians 6:13)

As a Servant, you also have a specific function for which you'll be evaluated and paid wages at the end of your service.

What is this function?

First, let's understand that the words "servant" and "minister" are interchangeable… they mean the same thing.

A Servant is a Minister - A Minister is a Servant, therefore, every Born Again Christian is a Minister of God.

That doesn't necessarily mean you are called to function in one of the 5-fold Ministry Offices of the Apostle, Prophet, Pastor, Teacher, or Evangelist, but you are called to be a

Minister nonetheless.

Ministry in the Body of Christ is two-fold:

Every Christian has a basic ministry and a specific ministry.

Concerning your specific ministry, you might be called to be a Pastor, a Prophet, or a Teacher or you may be called to be a Doctor, a Musician, or a Carpenter.

Some Christians are called to be Parents... that's it.

There is no higher call than to be the personal shepherd of another human soul... which is to be a Parent!

As someone's mother or father, you represent God to that person, especially in their very early years.

There is no greater honor than to represent God to a child.

Jesus said, "These little ones believe in me. It would be best for the person who causes one of them to lose faith to be thrown into the sea with a large stone hung around his neck."
Mark 9:42 (GWT)

The Parent/Child relationship is the foundation and framework for the God/Adult relationship.

A child's perception of their parents, particularly their father, strongly frames their perception of God.

The kind of person our father was and how he treated us is how we expect God to be and treat us.

God told Moses, "Bring the people of Israel here. I want to speak to them so they will obey me as long as they live, and so they will teach their children to obey me too." Deuteronomy 4:10 (CEV)

God was setting an example as a Parent.

Whether your specific calling is to be a Pastor, a Plumber, or a Parent, we are commanded to do it as though we are working directly for Jesus Christ.

The Bible says, "Bondservants, obey your earthly masters with fear and trembling, with a sincere heart, as you would Christ." Ephesians 6:5 (ESV)

NOTE: In the Kingdom of God you are not rewarded for your title or position, so it doesn't matter whether you are called to be a Pastor or a Plumber.

Your rewards in Heaven are based on how you fulfilled your office, not the title of your position.

So, an outstanding Christian Plumber will be **rewarded greater** in the Kingdom of God than a lousy Pastor.

That's how the Kingdom of God works!

Apart from your specific calling, however, there is also a basic ministry that every Believer has.

The Ministry of Reconciliation

The basic Ministry for all Christians is the Ministry of Reconciliation.

The essence of reconciliation is… making peace with God.

The Bible says, "All these things are from God, who reconciled us to Himself through Christ [making us acceptable to Him] and gave us the ministry of reconciliation [so that by our example we might bring others to Him]." 2nd Corinthians 5:18 (AMP)

Reconciliation is, the restoring of a broken relationship between those who were once closely related but found themselves opposing each other.

It involves the resolving and dissolving of enmity between estranged parties.

Reconciliation means the complete removal of barriers that stood between you and God, so you can be reunited in peace.

Our chief function as Servants of God is to accurately and effectively represent Christ to others, so they can be reconciled to God and enjoy a fruitful relationship with Him.

We are expected at all times to cultivate holy character and demonstrate godly conduct.

The Bible teaches us that, "The servant of the Lord must not participate in quarrels, but must be kind to everyone [even-tempered, preserving peace, and must be], skilled in teaching, patient and tolerant when wronged." 2nd Timothy 2:24 (AMP)

The Ministry of Reconciliation also has it's rewards.

If we effectively represent Christ by our lifestyle we will qualify for different ranks and rewards in the Kingdom of God.

Jesus said, "Behold, I am coming quickly, and My reward is with Me, to reward each one as his work deserves." Revelation 22:12 (NASB)

The Bible says, "God blesses those who patiently endure testing and temptation. Afterward they will receive the crown of life." James 1:12 (NLT)

Paul, the Apostle said, "There is laid up for me the crown of righteousness, which the Lord, the righteous Judge, will give to me on that Day." 2nd Timothy 4:8

Jesus said, "To the one who is victorious I will give the right to sit with me on my throne. And "To the one who is victorious and does my will to the end, I will give authority over the nations." Revelation 3:21 and Revelation 2:26 (NIV)

In this verse, "doing His will" simply means fulfilling both your specific and your basic ministries with excellence.

We can easily condense all of these instructions into one, "Imitate God, therefore, in everything you do, because you are his dear children." Ephesians 5:1 (NLT)

To do His will is simply to imitate God and do everything His way.

At the Judgment Seat of Christ, we will gain or lose rewards based on how well we represented Christ to others here on earth.

Please understand, this does not mean you have to go door to door telling everyone about Jesus nor stand on a street corner with a microphone preaching the Gospel.

There is nothing wrong with doing either of these activities but not everyone is specifically called to do them.

Representing Christ means doing your best in consistently thinking, speaking, and acting like Him in every situation and circumstance.

I knew a Man of God called, Brother Pope who was completely paralyzed from his shoulders down.

He was bedridden and depended on others to do everything for him but every time we visited him he was beaming with joy, full of the Spirit of Christ.

Brother Pope was a beacon of light and joy to everyone who knew him and he drew others to Christ by his holy character.

He always had a smile and an encouraging word and you could tell it wasn't some show he was putting on because you could feel it deep on the inside, you knew this was real, the Spirit of Christ palpably emanated from him.

I have no doubt his reward in heaven is great.

There are Christians who might devote their lives to prayer and fasting for the unsaved, who never personally led anyone to Christ but did exactly what the Holy Spirit led them to do... *just pray!*

They will be greatly rewarded in heaven as well.

In serving God, one of the most important things to remember is... God rewards obedience, not activity.

Entering vs Inheriting the Kingdom

Many believers are extremely busy, doing stuff for their local church, they're involved in every committee and every church program but are not doing the one thing God called them to do.

These Christians will not be rewarded for any of their activities outside the will of God because they're walking in disobedience.

Others are following God's instructions but in their own way, in their own time, and according to their own agenda, not realizing that... *partial obedience is total disobedience.*

They have zero inheritance for any deeds done in defiance of God's will.

King Saul of Israel is a perfect example of partial obedience and it's consequences.

God told him, "Go and completely destroy the entire Amalekite nation—men, women, children, babies, cattle, sheep, goats, camels, and donkeys." 1st Samuel 15:3 (NLT)

Saul decided he knew better than God as to what should be done so he spared King Agag and the best of the animals to sacrifice to God. (1st Samuel 15:9)

God rebuked him through the prophet Samuel saying, "What is more pleasing to the Lord: your burnt offerings and sacrifices or your obedience to his voice? Listen! Obedience is better than sacrifice, and submission is better than offering the fat of rams.

Rebellion is as sinful as witchcraft, and stubbornness as bad as worshiping idols.

So because you have rejected the command of the Lord, he has rejected you as king." 1st Samuel 15:22-23 (NLT)

Saul incurred the wrath of Almighty God and lost his entire kingdom because of partial obedience.

As an illustration, if I am teaching you to swim and I say, do exactly as I do, then I proceed to swim from the shallow end of the pool to the deep end, eventually reaching the far side and holding on to the side of the pool and resting.

You, however, follow me 99% of the way, swimming to the far end but never holding on to the side and resting.

What will eventually happen to you if you never hold on to the side and rest?

You will drown.

That's a simple illustration of what happens when you **do not** obey God 100%.

The Amalekites were completely saturated in satanism and sorcery, therefore, demonic possession was rampant throughout their tribes, infecting everyone, even the livestock.

In addition to this, according to Jewish tradition in the Midrash, the Amalekites were sorcerers who could transform themselves to resemble animals to avoid capture, hence another possible reason God commanded the livestock to be destroyed as well.

While we do not equate any traditional writings with the Holy Scriptures, the Midrash does seem to corroborate what history says about the sorcery practiced by these heathens.

The point is, God may not reveal His full mind to us when issuing a command, however, He still expects 100% obedience from us, and absolutely deserves it.

Partial obedience means total disobedience and will not be rewarded in the Kingdom of God.

The Bible says, "For this you know with certainty, that no sexually immoral or impure or greedy person, which amounts to an idolater, has an inheritance in the kingdom of Christ and God." Ephesians 5:5 (NASB)

The works of the flesh listed in Galatians 5:19-21 give a much longer list of those disobedient Christians who will not share in the inheritance of those Christians who live and walk in holiness and godliness.

There is a difference between *entering* the Kingdom of God and *inheriting* the Kingdom of God.

Not every child of a wealthy man gets to inherit his wealth, only those he specifically selects in his will, only those who show themselves worthy to manage his wealth and lead his empire.

As it is naturally... so it is spiritually.

Not every Child of God gets to inherit His Kingdom.

To inherit God's kingdom is to reign and rule with Christ in glory.

Only Servants of God who cultivate the character of Christ will form part of the Government of God and rule with Christ.

Reigning and ruling with Him is a promise Jesus makes specifically to those who overcome, i.e. who consistently walk in the manifestation of their God-given victory.

Being handed victory is one thing, laying hold on that victory and walking in the fullness of it is something entirely different.

As Christians, Titus 3:5 tells us we are saved, but Philippians 2:12 still admonishes us to work out our salvation with fear and trembling and 1st Timothy 6:12 still tells us to lay hold on eternal life.

Why would the Bible command us to "lay hold on eternal life" if salvation is permanent and cannot be lost? It's because even though we are permanently saved it still matters *how* we live our lives after becoming born again.

Laying hold on eternal life means walking in the fullness of the divine life Jesus died to give you.

This is worship... such a life brings honor and glory to God.

At the end of our time on earth there will be an evaluation of how we used our salvation.

You've heard it said that salvation is free but it's not cheap.

Someone literally died to give you the life you now enjoy, and with that new life comes a responsibility.

Stan Lee was right, "With great power does come great responsibility."

There is no greater power given to men than to have the Creator of the Universe living inside you and ready to work with you.

In several places the Bible tells us that we have great power with God.

It says, "Thus says the LORD... concerning the work of My hands, you command Me." Isaiah 45:11

"Truly I tell you, whatever you bind on earth will be bound in heaven, and whatever you loose on earth will be loosed in heaven." Matthew 18:18 (BSB)

"Behold, I have given you authority to tread on snakes and scorpions, and over all the power of the enemy. Nothing will harm you." Luke 10:19 (BSB)

"And whatever you might ask in My name, this I will do, so that the Father may be glorified in the Son." John 14:13 (BSB)

Every Born Again Believer who distinguishes themself by demonstrating holy character and godly conduct will reign and rule with Jesus Christ when He returns to Earth in His Glory.

Every other Believer will still be citizens of the Kingdom of God but will not rule as leaders, they will not form part of God's Government.

That's why Jesus wrote to the 7 churches and strongly admonished them, "to the one who is victorious I will give the right to sit with me on my throne and "to the one who is victorious and does my will to the end, I will give authority over the nations." Revelation 3:21 and Revelation 2:26 (NIV)

Only those Christians who approve themselves by holy character and godly living, who lived as victorious overcomers will be granted the right to form part of Jesus' Government on Earth when He returns.

Ask yourself this, when Jesus returns to rule the world, as King of kings and Lord of lords, who are these other kings and lords ruling with Him?

He is the King of other kings and the Lord of other lords… who are they?

They are Christians who have cultivated holy character and godly conduct, accurately and effectively representing Christ to their friends, family, neighbors, co-workers, classmates, etc.

Our character determines our conduct and our conduct determines how we'll be received when we enter heaven… as victorious overcomers or unprofitable servants, fit for Outer Darkness.

7

Heavenly Mansions vs. Outer Darkness

There are two biblical concepts, which reveal how Jesus deals with faithful vs. unfaithful servants **or** spiritual vs. carnal Christians in heaven.

They are:

1. **Heavenly Mansions**
2. **Outer Darkness**

The concept of faithful servants of God being rewarded with Mansions in heaven is detailed in John 14 and the concept of unprofitable servants being cast into Outer Darkness is detailed in Matthew 22 and 25.

Heavenly Mansions

Jesus said, "In my Father's house there are many mansions: if it were not so, I would have told you." John 14:2

This refers to the rewards of a Servant of God who dispenses their duties well.

In this verse, the word "house" in Greek is "oikia" (pronounced oy-kee'-ah) and means "household" and by extension "family."

The word, "mansions" is "mone" (pronounced 'mon-ay') and means "residence" (the act or the place).

Now follow me closely…

The meaning of the word "mansions" is "residence" but it can either be the *place* of residence or the *act* of residence.

For my 35 plus years as a Christian, I've always heard it taught as a place of residence, Christians are always referring to their "mansion in heaven" and the "keys to their mansion."

But does this really make sense?

In my Father's house are many mansions?

If a mansion, by definition is a very large house, how can there be many mansions in a house?

If we're honest, this scripture verse taken literally makes no sense at all, does it?

Even if we expand the meaning of the word 'house' to mean 'household' or 'family' it's still like fitting a square peg in a round hole.

There must be another explanation for this scripture verse and I believe what follows is an accurate interpretation.

The word "residence" really refers to the *act* of residence and not a place of residence.

You may be familiar with the terms, "a doctor in residence" or "a doctor completing her residency."

Here's some interesting information from the **World Book Dictionary:**

"Residence" means – The seat of some power or activity.

"Residency" means – The position of a doctor who continues practicing in a hospital after completing their internship.

"Resident" means – An official sent to live in a foreign land to represent their country.

It's within this context that Jesus made the statement, "In my Father's house there are many mansions." (John 14:2)

What He's saying is, "within the Family or Government of God, there are many official positions of authority."

Many "Residencies" are available. (God is a King and His Family forms His Government)

Right now on earth we are spiritual interns in ministry

(Government Officials in Training) and if we successfully complete our internship, when Jesus sets up His Government on Earth we will be His Ministers in Residence.

Do you see it?

In the government of God, there are many residencies (official positions of authority), stop fighting among yourselves for bigger congregations and titles just to be recognized by men (this makes no sense).

This is one message we can take away from this scripture verse.

Jesus is saying the qualified servant of God can occupy and function in any one of these official positions if they show themselves approved here and now.

He didn't stop there either, look at the following verses.

"I go to prepare a place for you. And if I go and prepare a place for you, I will come again, and receive you unto myself; that where I am, there you may be also." John 14:2-3

The word "place" is translated from the Greek word, "topos" and means "special position" so "to prepare a place" means "to prepare a special position."

The word "receive" is translated from the Greek word, "paralambano" and means "to assume an office," the word "unto" is translated from "pros" which means "by the side of" and the phrase "may be" is the Greek word "o" which means "should stand."

I'm not making this up, just check a **Strong's Concordance.**

So, "In my Father's house are many mansions: if it were not so, I would have told you. I go to prepare a place for you. And if I go and prepare a place for you, I will come again, and receive you unto myself; that where I am, there you may be also."

Can be rightly interpreted as...

"There are many positions of authority in my Father's Government: If this weren't true I wouldn't say so. I'm leaving to prepare a special position for you. And if I'm doing this, then I will return and take you with me to stand in that position of authority at my side."

Bearing in mind, Jesus made this statement just after one of His ministers (Judas) left to betray Him and consequently abandon his official position in the Kingdom of God, the understanding is made clear.

Jesus is indicating to the rest of His ministers, that if in this life, they remain faithful to the ministry they are called and selected for, then after He returns, He will grant them the right to assume the official Governmental Offices in His Kingdom, for which they have been training.

Many Are Called - Few Are Chosen

Matthew 22:14 seals the deal when it says, "For many are called, but few are chosen." In this verse, being 'called' and 'chosen' is not about receiving salvation.

This verse has been largely misunderstood.

It's referring to the multitudes called to serve God on Earth and the few who endure the training that will qualify them to rule with Jesus in His Kingdom.

The word "called" from the Greek is "kletos" (pronounced 'klay-tos') meaning "invited" and the word "chosen" is "eklektos" (pronounced 'ek-lek-tos') meaning "selected."

There's a difference between being invited to occupy an office, and being selected to function in that office.

The phrase, "many are called but few are chosen" separates between spiritual and carnal Christians, between those who allow the Holy Spirit to train them to lead and those who remain contented to be followers all their lives.

Every Christian is called to be a minister, to serve in some capacity.

This doesn't mean everyone needs to be a Pastor or an Apostle.

A student who excels academically, while remaining submitted to her parents at home, who is a faithful friend and loving sister, who seeks to glorify God in all she does… this is a spiritual leader who will reap great rewards at the Judgment Seat of Christ and who will form part of the Government of God on Earth when Jesus returns.

A single mom working two jobs to make ends meet, who schedules time for prayer and fasting, who diligently teaches her kids the ways of God… this is a spiritual leader who will reap great rewards in the Kingdom of God and form part of the Government of God on Earth.

**God rewards character, not position, not title...
character!**

The Apostle or Prophet who was known worldwide and
adored by many but who abused his gifts and calling, taking
advantage of God's people **will not** rule in the Kingdom
of God.

The millionaire Pastor with a congregation of 25,000,
who graced Talk Shows and Magazine Covers, who authored
a multitude of Best-selling Books but who lived a secret life
of debauchery and disobedience despising the ways of God
will not form part of the Government of God when
Jesus returns.

Do you remember the difference between reputation
and character?

Your entire life of service today is nothing more than training
for the actual position of authority God has ordained for you
in His Kingdom.

That position is a divine office you will occupy during Jesus'
Millennial Reign (1000 Years) on Earth after he returns to rule
the world from Jerusalem.

The Bible says when Jesus returns, "In that day His feet
will stand on the Mount of Olives, which faces Jerusalem."
Zechariah 14:4

Then it says, "I saw thrones, and those who sat on them were
given the power to judge... and ruled as kings with Christ for a
thousand years." Revelation 20:4 (GNT)

Your decisions and actions today determine your quality of life tomorrow.

I urge you to read the entire Matthew Chapter 20 Parable of the Laborers in the Vineyard.

In it, Jesus highlighted the character of the workers, specifically those who had a bad attitude toward their job, toward their boss, and toward their co-workers.

The parable extends from verses 1 to 15 and in verse 16 Jesus says, "The last shall be first and the first last: for many are called but few chosen."

Of all the multitudes of God's Servants, there are relatively few who will patiently endure hardship, complete their training and qualify for their **Mansion in Heaven - Their Official Position of Authority in the Government of God.**

Those who do, will reign and rule as kings for 1000 years on earth with Jesus Christ, the King of kings.

Those carnal Christians who refuse to undergo the training of the Holy Spirit will still be citizens in Christ's Kingdom but they will not rule, nor form part of His Government.

Some of them may, in fact, experience what Jesus describes as Outer Darkness.

Outer Darkness

"Cast the unprofitable servant into outer darkness: there shall be weeping and gnashing of teeth." Matthew 25:30

Jesus made this statement after a very lengthy parable, demonstrating the difference between Servants of God who wisely invested their God-given resources and those who did not.

In Chapter Twenty-two of the same Gospel, He spoke of a guest at the wedding who had no wedding garment on, and for this, he was bound hand and foot, taken away and cast into outer darkness.

When we examine this passage from the original Greek, we get a much deeper understanding of what "Outer Darkness" really means.

. . . .

Special Note: As we continue discussing the word of God and we translate words from English to Greek, please do not be confused by this practice.

To accurately interpret God's word one can't just get a Strong's Concordance and begin translating words to form an opinion.

That's not the way this works.

The conclusions I share in this book are revelatory and based on my lifestyle of prayer, worship, fasting, and intimacy with the Holy Spirit, together with decades and decades of careful, prayerful Bible Study.

My conclusions come from aligning myself with the mind and heart of God, from hearing what He has to say and from receiving what he has deposited into my spirit to share with His People.

When I translate Bible words from English to Greek and reveal the underlying meaning, that is simply to confirm and clarify the revelation God has already given me and to accurately explain these revelations to you as simply as possible.

• • • • • • • •

Having shared that, let's look at some words from the Matthew Chapter 22 Parable in their original Greek to get a better understanding of what Jesus is saying to us.

The word "bind" from the Greek is "deo" meaning "to restrict", the word "hand" is "cheir" and means "power" and the word "foot" is "pous" translated as "footstool" which represents authority.

So, "to bind hand and foot," means, "to restrict in power and authority."

The Greek word translated "cast" is "ekballo" meaning "to expel," which means "to put a person out, to dismiss permanently."

The word "darkness" from the Greek is "skotos" meaning "obscurity."

So, through careful interpretation, we get the picture of someone who once belonged to a special group and was promised recognition and authority but who was permanently dismissed from that group, stripped of his power, and sentenced to a comparatively ordinary life.

This is what Matthew 22:13 is saying, "Bind him hand and foot, and take him away, and cast him into outer darkness;" can be interpreted as, "Restrict his ability and authority, banish him from this elite group and sentence him to a life of obscurity."

This is what happens to carnal Christians who fail to accurately and effectively represent God according to His standard of holiness.

Instead of recognition and reward for their labor of love, there will be loss and shame as they're permanently dismissed from the ranks of those who wisely invested their lives in godly service.

This is one revelation of Outer Darkness... it can be applied to a Christian who failed to be conformed to the image of Christ and lived only to please themselves.

Such a Christian is restricted in divine authority and ability and simply lives as an ordinary citizen in the kingdom of God.

He or she is denied the opportunity to form part of the Government of God on earth and share with Christ in His Kingly reign and glory.

This is evident in the parable of the servants who were given the pounds to invest in Luke 19:12-26, the one who did poorly was stripped of what he was given to invest and was denied any authority to rule, but the ones who did well were increased in authority and given more cities to rule over.

So, contrary to popular opinion, being cast into "outer darkness" has nothing to do with sinners being cast into Hell.

The final place of judgment for every unsaved person, including the devil and his demons is the Lake of Fire.

How can there be darkness in a Lake of Fire?

Outer Darkness cannot be hell and therefore, must be something else.

Outer Darkness is Not a Place... It's a Condition!

It is the specific consequence of the carnal Christian who refuses to follow God's plan for their life.

This is what happens to Christians who live like the world, who do not diligently follow the ways of God and accurately represent Christ to others.

Think about it...

Daniel 12:3 says "Those who are wise will shine like the brightness of the heavens, and those who lead many to righteousness, like the stars for ever and ever."

If living godly and fulfilling your divine purpose results in you reflecting the brightness and glory of God and being included in the government of God, what do you think living carnally results in?

How about a condition of outer darkness where you're excluded from God's government and will not reflect His Glory as you're meant to.

The Bible says, after we get to heaven God shall wipe away all tears from our eyes. (Revelation 21:4)

Here's a question... Why would we have sorrowful tears that God needs to wipe away *after* we get to heaven?

Well, when we stand before God in heaven and He evaluates our character and conduct on earth and we see all the missed opportunities we had to glorify Jesus and did not, I believe tears will flow.

When Jesus shows us how many times we failed Him and chose to glorify our flesh and how many times we selfishly put ourselves before others, I believe tears will flow.

When He shows us all the heavenly rewards we would have gotten and the position of authority we would have had in His

Kingdom but now will not, I believe tears will flow.

When we see how many of our friends and family members we could have brought with us to heaven and did not, and because of our selfishness they will now be cursing us as they burn forever in hell... our tears will definitely flow!

These are the tears He will wipe from our eyes before we finally enter into our full glory with Him.

"He will wipe every tear from their eyes, and there will be no more death or sorrow or crying or pain. All these things are gone forever." Revelation 21:4 (NLT)

Conclusion

Your nature determines *if* you enter heaven.

Your character determines *how* you enter heaven.

● ● ●

When you become Born Again and your spirit is transformed, your inner-most nature will be changed from merely human to also divine, and it is this new divine nature that guarantees you entrance into heaven and eternity with Jesus Christ.

● ● ●

When you renew your mind/soul and cultivate Christlike character and godly conduct, you will receive the rank and rewards God has prepared for you in His Kingdom.

Your holy character and godly conduct guarantees you will reign and rule with Jesus in His Kingdom when He returns to Earth.

● ● ●

"The kingdoms of this world have become the kingdoms of our Lord and of His Christ, and He shall reign forever and ever." Revelation 11:15

"For he is Lord of lords, and King of kings: and they that are with him are called, and chosen, and faithful." Revelation 17:14

Did you notice, Jesus is the King of other kings and the Lord of other lords?

Who are these other kings and lords?

They are the called and chosen, and faithful who are with Him.

They are the Christians who have victoriously overcome.

They are the few who are chosen from the many who are called.

They are those who fought the good fight of faith and patiently endured to the end.

They are those who laid hold on eternal life and worked out their salvation with fear and trembling.

They are those who took up their cross and followed Jesus daily.

They are you and I, who refuse to give up, give in or turn back, who persevere in the face of insurmountable odds, who press against the press, overcoming every obstacle in our path.

They are those of us who trust in the faithfulness of the God who promises to never leave us nor forsake us, who will be with us to the very end, empowering us to succeed.

They are you and I, who *know* that our salvation is Eternal, who practice holiness in the fear of the Lord, holiness which is built on the knowledge of this unshakable truth... that God loves us and can *never* be separated from us!

They are His Bride who will reign and rule with Jesus Christ on Earth, forming the Divine Government of God.

"Blessed (happy, prosperous, to be admired) and holy is the person who takes part in the first resurrection; over these the second death [which is eternal separation from God, the lake of fire] has no power or authority, but they will be priests of God and of Christ and they will reign with Him a thousand years." Revelation 20:6 (AMP)

Your regenerated spirit and divine nature guarantee you enter and live in the Kingdom and Presence of God.

Regeneration speaks to the salvation of your spirit.

Your renewed mind, holy character and godly conduct guarantee you inherit and rule in the Kingdom of God and of Christ.

Sanctification speaks to the salvation of your soul.

This is the difference, between your spirit and your soul.

~ The End ~

www.ingramcontent.com/pod-product-compliance
Lightning Source LLC
Chambersburg PA
CBHW060238030426
42335CB00014B/1508